JULIO CÉSAR CHÁVEZ

JULIO CÉSAR CHÁVEZ

Terrance Dolan

CHELSEA HOUSE PUBLISHERS

PHILADELPHIA

CHELSEA HOUSE PUBLISHERS

Editorial Director: Richard Rennert
Executive Managing Editor: Karyn Gullen Browne
Copy Chief: Robin James
Picture Editor: Adrian G. Allen
Art Director: Robert Mitchell
Manufacturing Director: Gerald Levine

HISPANICS OF ACHIEVEMENT
Senior Editor: Philip Koslow

Staff for *JULIO CÉSAR CHÁVEZ*
Copy Editor: Catherine Iannone
Editorial Assistant: Mary B. Sisson
Designer: M. Cambraia Magalhães
Picture Researcher: Sandy Jones
Cover Illustrator: Les Katz

3 5 7 9 8 6 4

Library of Congress Cataloging-in-Publication Data
Dolan, Terrance.
Julio César Chávez / Terrance Dolan.
p. cm.—(Hispanics of achievement)
0-7910-2021-5
0-7910-2022-3 (pbk.)
1. Chávez, Julio César—Juvenile literature. 2. Boxers (Sports)—Mexico—Biography—
Juvenile literature. [1. Chávez, Julio César. 2. Boxers (Sports)] I. Title. II. Series.
93-43867
GV1132.C52D65 1993
CIP
796.8'3'092—dc20
[B]
AC

CONTENTS

JOAN BAEZ
Mexican-American folksinger

RUBÉN BLADES
Panamanian lawyer and entertainer

JORGE LUIS BORGES
Argentine writer

PABLO CASALS
Spanish cellist and conductor

MIGUEL DE CERVANTES
Spanish writer

CESAR CHAVEZ
Mexican-American labor leader

JULIO CÉSAR CHÁVEZ
Mexican boxing champion

EL CID
Spanish military leader

HENRY CISNEROS
Mexican-American political leader

ROBERTO CLEMENTE
Puerto Rican baseball player

SALVADOR DALÍ
Spanish painter

PLÁCIDO DOMINGO
Spanish singer

GLORIA ESTEFAN
Cuban-American singer

GABRIEL GARCÍA MÁRQUEZ
Colombian writer

FRANCISCO JOSÉ DE GOYA
Spanish painter

JULIO IGLESIAS
Spanish singer

RAUL JULIA
Puerto Rican actor

FRIDA KAHLO
Mexican painter

JOSÉ MARTÍ
Cuban revolutionary and poet

RITA MORENO
Puerto Rican singer and actress

PABLO NERUDA
Chilean poet and diplomat

OCTAVIO PAZ
Mexican poet and critic

PABLO PICASSO
Spanish artist

ANTHONY QUINN
Mexican-American actor

DIEGO RIVERA
Mexican painter

LINDA RONSTADT
Mexican-American singer

ANTONIO LÓPEZ DE SANTA ANNA
Mexican general and politician

GEORGE SANTAYANA
Spanish philosopher and poet

JUNÍPERO SERRA
Spanish missionary and explorer

LEE TREVINO
Mexican-American golfer

PANCHO VILLA
Mexican revolutionary

CHELSEA HOUSE PUBLISHERS

HISPANICS OF ACHIEVEMENT

Rodolfo Cardona

The Spanish language and many other elements of Spanish culture are present in the United States today and have been since the country's earliest beginnings. Some of these elements have come directly from the Iberian Peninsula; others have come indirectly, by way of Mexico, the Caribbean basin, and the countries of Central and South America.

Spanish culture has influenced America in many subtle ways, and consequently many Americans remain relatively unaware of the extent of its impact. The vast majority of them recognize the influence of Spanish culture in America, but they often do not realize the great importance and long history of that influence. This is partly because Americans have tended to judge the Hispanic influence in the United States in statistical terms rather than to look closely at the ways in which individual Hispanics have profoundly affected American culture. For this reason, it is fitting that Americans obtain more than a passing acquaintance with the origins of these Spanish cultural elements and gain an understanding of how they have been woven into the fabric of American society.

It is well documented that Spanish seafarers were the first to explore and colonize many of the early territories of what is today called the United States of America. For this reason, students of geography discover Hispanic names all over the map of the United States. For instance, the Strait of Juan de Fuca was named after the Spanish explorer who first navigated the waters of the Pacific Northwest; the names of states such as Arizona (arid zone), Montana (mountain), Florida (thus named because it was reached on Easter Sunday, which in Spanish is called the feast of Pascua Florida), and California (named after a fictitious land in one of the first and probably the most popular among the Spanish novels of chivalry, *Amadis of Gaul*) are all derived from Spanish; and there are numerous mountains, rivers, canyons, towns, and cities with Spanish names throughout the United States.

Not only explorers but many other illustrious figures in Spanish history have helped define American culture. For example, the 13th-century king of Spain, Alfonso X, also known as the Learned, may be unknown to the majority of Americans, but his work on the codification of Spanish law has greatly influenced the evolution of American law, particularly in the jurisdictions of the Southwest. For this contribution a statue of him stands in the rotunda of the Capitol in Washington, D.C. Likewise, the name Diego Rivera may be unfamiliar to most Americans, but this Mexican painter influenced many American artists whose paintings, commissioned during the Great Depression and the New Deal era of the 1930s, adorn the walls of government buildings throughout the United States. In recent years the contributions of Puerto Ricans, Mexicans, Mexican Americans (Chicanos), and Cubans in American cities such as Boston, Chicago, Los Angeles, Miami, Minneapolis, New York, and San Antonio have been enormous.

The importance of the Spanish language in this vast cultural complex cannot be overstated. Spanish, after all, is second only to English as the most widely spoken of Western languages within the United States as well as in the entire world. The popularity of the Spanish language in America has a long history.

In addition to Spanish exploration of the New World, the great Spanish literary tradition served as a vehicle for bringing the language and culture to America. Interest in Spanish literature in America began when English immigrants brought with them translations of Spanish masterpieces of the Golden Age. As early as 1683, private libraries in Philadelphia and Boston contained copies of the first picaresque novel, *Lazarillo de Tormes*, translations of Francisco de Quevedo's *Los Sueños*, and copies of the immortal epic of reality and illusion *Don Quixote*, by the great Spanish writer Miguel de Cervantes. It would not be surprising if Cotton Mather, the arch-Puritan, read *Don Quixote* in its original Spanish, if only to enrich his vocabulary in preparation for his writing *La fe del cristiano en 24 artículos de la Institución de Cristo, enviada a los españoles para que abran sus ojos* (The Christian's Faith in 24 Articles of the Institution of Christ, Sent to the Spaniards to Open Their Eyes), published in Boston in 1699.

Over the years, Spanish authors and their works have had a vast influence on American literature—from Washington Irving, John Steinbeck, and Ernest Hemingway in the novel to Henry Wadsworth Longfellow and Archibald MacLeish in poetry. Such important American writers as James Fenimore Cooper, Edgar Allan Poe, Walt Whitman, Mark Twain, and Herman Melville all owe a sizable debt to the Spanish literary tradition. Some writers, such as Willa Cather and Maxwell Anderson, who explored Spanish themes they came into contact with in the American Southwest and Mexico, were influenced less directly but no less profoundly.

Important contributions to a knowledge of Spanish culture in the United States were also made by many lesser known individuals—teachers, publishers, historians, entrepreneurs, and others—with a love for Spanish culture. One of the most significant of these contributions was made by Abiel Smith, a Harvard College graduate of the class of 1764, when he bequeathed stock worth $20,000 to Harvard for the support of a professor of French and Spanish. By 1819 this endowment had produced enough income to appoint a professor, and the philologist and humanist George Ticknor became the first holder of the Abiel

Smith Chair, which was the very first endowed Chair at
Harvard University. Other illustrious holders of the Smith
Chair would include the poets Henry Wadsworth Longfellow
and James Russell Lowell.

A highly respected teacher and scholar, Ticknor was also a
collector of Spanish books, and as such he made a very special
contribution to America's knowledge of Spanish culture. He was
instrumental in amassing for Harvard libraries one of the first and
most impressive collections of Spanish books in the United States.
He also had a valuable personal collection of Spanish books and
manuscripts, which he bequeathed to the Boston Public Library.

With the creation of the Abiel Smith Chair, Spanish language
and literature courses became part of the curriculum at Harvard,
which also went on to become the first American university to
offer graduate studies in Romance languages. Other colleges and
universities throughout the United States gradually followed
Harvard's example, and today Spanish language and culture may
be studied at most American institutions of higher learning.

No discussion of the Spanish influence in the United States,
however brief, would be complete without a mention of the
Spanish influence on art. Important American artists such as John
Singer Sargent, James A. M. Whistler, Thomas Eakins, and Mary
Cassatt all explored Spanish subjects and experimented with
Spanish techniques. Virtually every serious American artist living
today has studied the work of the Spanish masters as well as the
great 20th-century Spanish painters Salvador Dalí, Joan Miró,
and Pablo Picasso.

The most pervasive Spanish influence in America, however,
has probably been in music. Compositions such as Leonard
Bernstein's *West Side Story*, the Latinization of William Shake-
speare's *Romeo and Juliet* set in New York's Puerto Rican quarter,
and Aaron Copland's *Salon Mexico* are two obvious examples. In
general, one can hear the influence of Latin rhythms—from
tango to mambo, from guaracha to salsa—in virtually every form
of American music.

This series of biographies, which Chelsea House has published under the general title HISPANICS OF ACHIEVEMENT, constitutes further recognition of—and a renewed effort to bring forth to the consciousness of America's young people—the contributions that Hispanic people have made not only in the United States but throughout the civilized world. The men and women who are featured in this series have attained a high level of accomplishment in their respective fields of endeavor and have made a permanent mark on American society.

The title of this series must be understood in its broadest possible sense: The term *Hispanics* is intended to include Spaniards, Spanish Americans, and individuals from many countries whose language and culture have either direct or indirect Spanish origins. The names of many of the people included in this series will be immediately familiar; others will be less recognizable. All, however, have attained recognition within their own countries, and often their fame has transcended their borders.

The series HISPANICS OF ACHIEVEMENT thus addresses the attainments and struggles of Hispanic people in the United States and seeks to tell the stories of individuals whose personal and professional lives in some way reflect the larger Hispanic experience. These stories are exemplary of what human beings can accomplish, often against daunting odds and by extraordinary personal sacrifice, where there is conviction and determination. Fray Junípero Serra, the 18th-century Spanish Franciscan missionary, is one such individual. Although in very poor health, he devoted the last 15 years of his life to the foundation of missions throughout California—then a mostly unsettled expanse of land—in an effort to bring a better life to Native Americans through the cultivation of crafts and animal husbandry. An example from recent times, the Mexican-American labor leader Cesar Chavez battled bitter opposition and made untold personal sacrifices in his effort to help poor agricultural workers who have been exploited for decades on farms throughout the Southwest.

The talent with which each one of these men and women may have been endowed required dedication and hard work to develop and become fully realized. Many of them have enjoyed rewards for their efforts during their own lifetime, whereas others have died poor and unrecognized. For some it took a long time to achieve their goals, for others success came at an early age, and for still others the struggle continues. All of them, however, stand out as people whose lives have made a difference, whose achievements we need to recognize today and should continue to honor in the future.

JULIO CÉSAR CHÁVEZ

THE NEW FIRE

Julio César Chávez raises his arms in triumph after knocking out Angel Hernández in Mexico City on April 10, 1992, raising his record to 80-0. With the victory, Chávez retained his World Boxing Council (WBC) super-lightweight title.

During the night, Aztec priests climbed a hill near Tenochtitlán and, exactly at midnight, sacrificed an enemy warrior by cutting out his heart. Then they kindled the 'new fire' in the chest cavity of the sacrificed captive. If the fire flamed up, it was a sign that the universe would continue for another 52 years. This fire lit torches carried by the fastest runners to light all the torches and hearths at temples, schools, and houses. . . . This ritual took place with the entire population looking on anxiously." Thus does anthropologist Frances F. Berdan describe the Aztec new fire ritual, which took place in the 15th-century metropolis of Tenochtitlán, the capital of the great Aztec empire and the site of modern-day Mexico City.

Tenochtitlán was one of the most magnificent cities in the world, with a population numbering upwards of 200,000. Five centuries or so later, on the night of February 20, 1993, 132,274 citizens of Mexico City, most of whom could—and frequently do—boast proudly of their Aztec ancestry, were jammed into Estadio Azteca (Aztec Stadium) to, in effect, do the same thing that their Aztec forefathers had done on the night of the new fire ritual: watch a high priest cut the heart out of a sacrificial enemy warrior. One hundred thirty thousand people might have been a disappointing turnout for a human sacrifice in old

Tenochtitlán, when the entire populace would show up for the event, but it would be hard to cram contemporary Mexico City's population of 25 million into Aztec Stadium. Outside, filling the streets surrounding the arena, thousands had enjoyed a day-long fiesta. And those millions of Mexicans who did not converge on Aztec Stadium that night gathered everywhere—in the hotels along the Reforma, the grand boulevard of the central city where the foundations of Aztec structures are still apparent beneath the stately old-world Spanish buildings; in the Zócalo, the great city's central square; in the crowded bars of the Plaza Garibaldi, where on this evening the nightly mariachi music gave way to television and radio coverage of the event; in living rooms of houses throughout the sprawling suburbs; on the corners of the narrow, labyrinthine streets and in the networks of alleys in the poor sections of town; and in the teeming shanty-towns where the truly impoverished struggle for survival—shantytowns built on, and of, the tons of refuse produced daily by the metropolis. They gathered to watch on televisions or movie screens, to listen on radios, or, lacking either, to wait for word of mouth. They waited, in effect, for the "torches carried by the fastest runners" to bring them news of the bloody event; as if indeed the next 52 years of the universe hung in the balance.

The "Aztec priest," in this case, was Mexican prizefighter Julio César Chávez. Chávez had been cutting the hearts out of opponents for the past 13 years. At the age of 30, he was, simply put, the best professional boxer in the world, and he had established himself as one of the best in the history of the sport. His record was unprecedented—87 victories, 75 of them by knockout, and *no defeats;* 24 victories in championship fights; 17 by knockout. Chávez had won five championship titles in three weight divisions—super featherweight, lightweight, and super lightweight (also known as junior welterweight). He was currently the reigning World Boxing Council (WBC) super-lightweight champion. He had never been knocked down in the ring—he appeared to possess what boxing people call an iron jaw. And, at a mere 140 pounds, he was the most physically destructive prizefighter currently active.

To say that 130,000 Mexicans crowded into Aztec Stadium to see Chávez cut the heart out of an enemy warrior in a ritual ceremony is not simply a metaphor. In boxing terms, to "take away an opponent's heart" is to inflict such punishment on him that he no longer has the emotional or physical will, or "heart," to continue fighting. This has always been Julio César Chávez's game. His relentless, methodical assaults on his adversary's midsection—the crux of his attack in the ring—kindle an agonizing and often unendurable fire in the opponent's chest cavity, ribs, liver, abdomen, and groin area. Along with his short, chopping uppercuts, hammering left hooks, synapse-scrambling overhand rights, and stiff, merciless left jabs to the face and head—all thrown with a daunting force and accuracy, and most often thrown in combinations of two, three, four, and even five blows at a time—Chávez's attack burns away a fighter's heart, sometimes permanently. The list of talented boxers who, as it is often repeated, "have never been the same" after going 8, 10, or 12 rounds with Chávez is somewhat frightening, for they are, or were, skilled, hard-hitting, resilient, champion-caliber boxers, some of whom possessed superb defensive capabilities—Mario Martínez, Edwin Rosario, Juan LaPorte, and Meldrick Taylor. (Boxers of lesser talent who have faced Chávez, oddly enough, escape this kind of long-lasting damage, for they are invariably knocked cold in the first two or three rounds and are thus spared 10 or 12 rounds on the receiving end of Chávez's punches.) The famed trainer Angelo Dundee, who manned Muhammad Ali's corner throughout the great one's career, and who trained multititle champion Sugar Ray Leonard, among others, has been watching, with his expert eye, boxers good, bad, and great come and go for 40 years. Of Julio César Chávez, Dundee says, simply: "The toughest fighter I have ever seen, bar none."

Certainly 32-year-old Greg Haugen, Chávez's opponent that night, did not think of himself as a human sacrifice; at least not before he entered the stadium and climbed down to the ring. Nor did Chávez or his legions perceive anything symbolic in Greg Haugen, initially. Haugen was to be just another opponent, another victim to be climbed over as Chávez moved inexorably toward prizefighting immortality. For the most part, the opponents of Chávez, regardless of nationality, were irrelevant, for they all suffered the same fate. The evening at Aztec Stadium was intended to be a celebration of Chávez and of Mexico—a grand fiesta and a tribute to the man who had become Mexico's national hero. But then Greg Haugen started talking.

Whether he was in the throes of a fit of machismo or whether it was some fantastically ill-conceived strategic maneuver intended to infuriate Chávez and disrupt his concentration, Haugen's comments managed to insult not only Chávez but the entire populace of Mexico. What finally turned Haugen from mere opponent to candidate for a ritual vivisection was the fact that his prefight comments managed to do something that few fighters, and indeed, few people in general, have managed to do—they made Julio César Chávez mad.

132,274 people—the largest paying audience in boxing history—fill Mexico City's giant Aztec Stadium on February 20, 1993, to witness the bout between Chávez and Greg Haugen. The fight was a tremendous event in Mexico, in part because of Haugen's insulting comments about Chávez and Mexicans in general.

Ironically, Greg Haugen was a fighter with a reputation for having "a lot of heart"; he was fond of reminding people that he had never failed to finish any bout during his professional career. If he only had a brain, as the scarecrow character in *The Wizard of Oz* lamented, he might have been more judicious in his comments before the fight. Going into the contest with Chávez, Haugen had a record of 33 wins, 4 losses, and a draw. He had enjoyed a brief stint as International Boxing Federation (IBF) lightweight champion. Haugen was known as a tough guy and an excellent counterpuncher who adapted well to his opponents' style. He trained hard and fought hard, although he was not known as a particularly powerful hitter. What he most needed in preparation for his bout with Chávez, however, was a lesson in history—international history as well as prizefighting history.

Before the fight, hearing that Don King, promoter and Chávez's manager, expected a sellout crowd at Aztec Stadium, Haugen was quoted as saying that there "ain't 130,000 Mexicans in the whole world who can afford $1.65 to see this fight." Ticket prices ranged from $1.50 for the high-altitude seats at the top of the massive stadium (the price included a pair of cheap binoculars, although huge closed-circuit screens were set up above the ring as well), to $900 for seats on the infield. Haugen's comment rankled Mexicans everywhere. Mexico's relationship with its large, wealthy, and powerful neighbor to the north has been a troubled one at best since September 1847, when General Winfield Scott led a vastly outnumbered U.S. Army into Mexico and captured Mexico City, annexing fully one-third of sovereign Mexican territory in the process—present-day Texas, Utah, California, New Mexico, Nevada, Arizona, and Colorado. Mexicans have harbored a simmering resentment toward the United States ever since, and subsequent U.S. incursions into their territory, as well as the perennial political, economic, and cultural friction between the two nations, have not helped matters. Today's Mexicans are well aware that they are looked down upon by many Americans. Haugen's remarks were a perfect example of the nature of the racist stereotyping of Mexicans and Mexican immigrants that exists in the United States today.

Having insulted Mexico, Haugen compounded his troubles by personally insulting Chávez. Referring to his opponent's spectacular record, Haugen commented that most of Chávez's earlier fights were against "Tijuana taxi drivers." Haugen was implying that Chávez had padded his record by fighting a lot of "bums," or boxers of little talent. Chávez, to say the least, was offended. As with most other professional sports today, a certain amount of "talking trash" comes with the territory. Boxing promoters often encourage this in order to stir up fan interest and bolster ticket sales. Just about every noted fighter who has challenged Chávez has boasted of how he was going to be the fighter to finally put a loss on Chávez's record. Chávez, for the most part, is impervious to such babble, as long as it does not get too personal. It usually bothers him about as much as a mediocre left jab. Those fighters who had previously managed to insult Chávez had paid a high price for their indiscretions. Rubén Castillo, who was thoroughly mangled by Chávez during a title bout in 1985, has this advice for future adversaries of Chávez: "The best thing to do against Chávez is don't get him mad. Like, for instance, Haugen. I mean, it's idiotic and crazy to make a guy like Chávez angry. I mean, you're gonna get your ass kicked anyway. . . . But if he's angry at you, good grief!"

Chávez might have shrugged off Haugen's comments about his record. But the American fighter's remarks about Mexicans in general could not be ignored. Chávez enjoys a relationship with his countrymen and -women that is unprecedented in sports history. With the possible exceptions of U.S. baseball legend Joe DiMaggio, Brazil's preternaturally gifted soccer star Pelé, and the French skier Jean-Claude Killy, no athlete has been so unconditionally revered in his or her nation. There are songs about Chávez; the red headband Chávez traditionally wears into the ring is worn across Mexico by schoolchildren and businessmen alike. As far as Mexicans are concerned, Julio César Chávez *is* Mexico—he is the embodiment of Mexico's pride, its hope, and its dreams; the vindicator of a national history in which Mexico has suffered repeated conquest and humiliation by invaders and centuries of internal bloodshed, corruption, and betrayal of its heroes; and the two-fisted response to the notions of superiority that flow down across the border from *El Norte*.

Chávez's deep anger toward Haugen was evident in his own prefight remarks, which were uncharacteristically nasty. Chávez seldom has anything to say at all about his opponent before a fight. He disdains macho trash talking. Outside the ring, the word that is most often used to describe him is *gentleman*. But his response to Haugen's remarks was anything but gentlemanly. He promised to administer "una paliza mala" (a bad beating) to Haugen. At a prefight press conference, Chávez went further, saying, in Spanish, "I despise that son of a [prostitute]." King, translating for American reporters, was asked what Chávez had said. He gave a somewhat edited version of Chávez's remark: "Julio dislikes him strongly."

Haugen may have been unaware of American and Mexican history and of Chávez's ring history, or he may have chosen to ignore them. But he could not ignore the history that was made inside Aztec Stadium on the night of the fight, where 132,274 spectators had filled the massive arena to its brim. It was the largest paying crowd in boxing history, surpassing the previous record of the 120,470 who had gathered to see the first battle between legendary heavyweight champion Jack Dempsey and his nemesis Gene Tunney in Philadelphia in 1926.

The size of the crowd in Aztec Stadium was yet another promotional triumph for Don King, especially considering the fact that no heavyweight championship was involved. King is a unique character. With his electric-chair hairdo and creative, if not outright bizarre, use of the English language, he seems more suited to the antics of the professional wrestling business or a traveling carnival than to prizefighting.

(The Japanese, who became acquainted with King when the promoter brought Mike Tyson to Japan for his fateful fight with Buster Douglas, and who display an ongoing fascination for the more extreme and arcane manifestations of American culture, quickly became obsessed with King, whom they refer to as "he of the most frightening hairdo.") Don King is universally despised by the predominantly white sports media in the United States. He has a suspect reputation as a manager—King is constantly being sued by former clients and investigated by everyone from Congress to the FBI—but as a promoter, the giant, comically loquacious, Gumby-like figure has no equal. Among his past promotional coups were the "Rumble in the Jungle"—the championship bout between George Foreman and Muhammad Ali staged in Kinshasa, Zaire,

Chávez walks toward his corner in the fifth round as a bruised and battered Greg Haugen slumps to the canvas. "I could have ended it right away," Chávez said after the bout, "but for what he said about my people, I wanted him to suffer."

Africa, in October 1974; and the "Thrilla in Manilla" grudge match between Ali and his archnemesis Joe Frazier in Manila, the Philippines, in October 1975.

As night fell over Aztec Stadium on February 20, 1993, the atmosphere inside the arena became surreal, as if it were a scene from a magical realist novel by one of Latin America's contemporary writers. The temperature was pleasantly moderate; evening winds had dispersed the bubble of smog that usually envelops Mexico City like the green dome that encapsulates the fictional city of Oz. Stars appeared in the clear sky—a rarity above Mexico City. The ringside seats on the infield were separated from the rest of the arena by a moat, which was enclosed by barbed wire and patrolled by riot police with attack dogs and assault rifles. One thousand five hundred helmeted and heavily armed paramilitaries were in evidence throughout the stadium. Helicopters buzzed overhead, sweeping the stadium with blinding searchlights. A spectacular laser light show added to the fantastic scene. Don King was ecstatic. "Estupendo!" he declared, waving his arms about as laser light ignited his towering hairdo with blinding colors. "Magnífico! Fantástico!" The crowd, however, was remarkably orderly—even when several scantily clad female dancers in neo-Aztec/Las Vegas–style outfits performed between the three preliminary bouts.

Finally, the main event was at hand. Greg Haugen entered the ring first. Amazingly, he seemed intent on pushing the American-versus-Mexican scenario to the limits. He made his way to the ring with Bruce Springsteen's "Born in the U.S.A." blaring over the loudspeakers. Haugen was wearing a stars-and-stripes warm-up suit that made him look like an actor playing Davy Crockett in a third-rate film version of the Battle of the Alamo (apparently Haugen had forgotten or was unaware that the Texans had in fact been defeated by the Mexican army at the Alamo—for him, "Remember the Alamo," the subsequent battle cry of vengeful Texans, would have served better as words of caution than as a war cry). Members of his entourage waved U.S. flags. Such an entrance, especially after the comments Haugen had made, might very well have resulted in an ugly reaction from the crowd. But the 130,000 Mexicans in attendance reacted to Haugen's silly display with waves of derisive laughter. They would let Chávez take care of this gringo.

Julio César Chávez arrived from above, by helicopter. He made his way down through the crowd to the ring, passing amid a sea of hands that reached for a mere touch of his robe. The low rumble that had been building in anticipation of his appearance now grew to thunderous proportions. In Nahuatl, the old Aztec language, the Valley of Mexico was known as "land of the shaking earth," a reference to the earthquakes that have rocked that region for centuries. And as Chávez climbed through the ropes into the ring, wearing a robe decorated with images of Our Lady of Guadalupe on the back and an eagle clutching a serpent in its beak—the symbol of modern-day Mexico as well as of Mexico's Aztec heritage—on the front, the roar of the immense crowd achieved seismic proportions. The ritual was about to begin.

guzmã. michvacã.

"O MY BELOVED SONS!"

One night in Tenochtitlán, the new fire failed to kindle. The Aztec high priests assured the Aztec emperor Montezuma and the people of the empire that, nevertheless, all was well; the gods had been offended for some transgression, but they would be appeased by the correct rituals and sacrifices.

But the people and the emperor were fearful. Rumors of strange portents in the sky and omens of impending catastrophe swept through the empire. It was said that the waters of Lake Texcoco, which surrounded the island-capital of Tenochtitlán, had boiled like a great cauldron one night. An eerie, fiery light burned in the sky over the city each night for a year. Old men and women began reporting that they were all experiencing the same dreams. In the dreams, they saw visions of fires consuming the temples and pyramids of Tenochtitlán, which crumbled as if from a terrible earthquake, "and the great chieftains and lords filled with fright, abandoning the city and fleeing toward the hills." Most frightening of all was the apparition of a wailing old woman that appeared in the silent predawn hours, shrieking, "O my beloved sons, now we are about to go!" As the omens continued, many of the Aztecs believed that the end of the world was approaching. They were right.

A 16th-century drawing of Aztec warriors battling conquistadores and their Mexican-Indian allies. A new, distinct Mexican culture eventually emerged from the blending of Spanish and native Mexican traditions..

For the Aztec empire, and for the majority of indigenous native-Mexican cultures, the end of the world came in the year 1519. When it was reported to Montezuma that strange-looking "mounds" had appeared on the ocean off the east coast of Mexico, the emperor believed that Quetzalcoatl had returned from the sea to reclaim his domain. According to Aztec mythology, Quetzalcoatl, the powerful and ancient god who had given the gifts of maize (corn), art, and learning to the Aztecs, had left Mexico sometime in the distant past. The god, who was represented in Aztec art by a winged serpent, had gone off over the ocean but had promised to return and assume divine rule over Mexico. The mounds, Montezuma thought, must surely signal the return of the god from across the ocean, and thus the end of the world as the Aztecs knew it and the start of a new age.

The mounds drawing near to the Mexican coast were in fact the sailing ships of the Spanish Conquest. They carried conquistadores—the adventurer-warriors of the Spanish Empire. For sheer military bravado, Spain's conquistadores have no equal in the annals of history. These 15th- and 16th-century shock troops were expert, cunning, and savage fighters. They cannot be described as merely fearless, for as they hacked and blasted their way across Central and South America in the name of God and the Crown (and, more to the point, in the name of gold, silver, and any other riches that might be plundered in the New World), they frequently found themselves in situations in which they were vastly outnumbered by huge native armies bent on annihilating the invaders. What separated the conquistadores from other fighting forces was their response to fear—they typically reacted to such situations with a homicidal fury. In November 1532, for example, a force of 160 conquistadores led by Francisco Pizarro butchered an army of several thousand

Inca warriors at Cajamarca, Peru—an event that signaled the downfall of the Inca empire of South America. Apparently, not a single Spaniard was killed in the combat. This lust for battle, along with a military and psychological advantage afforded by steel weapons, horses, huge and vicious mastiffs, and firearms—none of which the native South and Central Americans had ever seen before—provided the conquistadores with a terrifying aura for peoples such as the Incas and the Aztecs (not to mention various tribes of what is now the American Southwest).

The Spanish ships were soon anchored off present-day Veracruz, and a force of conquistadores was marching inland toward Tenochtitlán. They were led by one of the most famous of all conquistadores: Hernán Cortés. Hungry for power, cynical, guileful, vengeful, immoral, and singularly brutal—even by conquistador standards—Cortés was motivated primarily by one thing: what he himself called "a disease of the heart, the lust for gold." Cortés had heard of the marvelous city of the Aztecs and the riches to be found there—a conquistador's dream come true—and he lost no time in organizing an invasionary expedition to Tenochtitlán.

"Now we are about to go!" the old woman in the dream had wailed in the streets of Tenochtitlán at night, but the Aztecs did not go easily. They were themselves among the fiercest of warriors, renowned and feared throughout the Valley of Mexico for their military prowess. The Aztec empire and culture itself, despite its more sublime attributes such as its awe-inspiring architecture and art, its sophisticated science, and its remarkable codices and calendar systems, had been established and maintained through force of arms and military intimidation. Those peoples of the Valley of Mexico who had been subjugated by the Aztecs were relegated to slavery or forced to pay tribute to their conquerors, and the Aztecs' notorious rituals of human sacrifice—at times thousands of captured enemy soldiers would be sacrificed over a period of days—were used as much to keep the conquered tribes in line through sheer terror as they were to appease the pantheon of hungry Aztec gods and goddesses.

Emperor Montezuma, however, was not the most decisive of men to be in charge when his empire and the entire Aztec culture were faced with the threat of these strange and savage invaders from across the ocean. He could not decide whether Cortés was indeed Quetzalcoatl or simply a bearded, pale-skinned, strangely attired variety of humanity. Meanwhile, as Cortés and his troops marched inland, their mouths

An engraving of the conquest of the Aztec empire in 1521 by Hernán Cortés and his troops. Cortés was aided by horses, superior weapons, and the Aztecs' many enemies among the tribes of the Valley of Mexico.

watering as they listened to tales of the magnificent city that lay ahead, Cortés was shrewdly allying himself with the enemies of the Aztecs. The most formidable of these were the Tlaxcalans, one of the few peoples of the Valley of Mexico who had never been defeated by the Aztecs. The conquistadores and the Tlaxcalans greeted one another by waging a battle; when the Tlaxcalans got a bloody taste of the conquistadores' swords and lances, they prudently joined forces with Cortés.

When the conquistadores and their Tlaxcalan escort arrived at Tenochtitlán and marched across the spectacular causeways over the lake and into the inner city, Montezuma, still unsure of the nature of Cortés, welcomed them all as guests, despite the long enmity between the Tlaxcalans and the Aztecs. This was much like inviting wolves into the sheeps' pen. The emperor's "guests" wasted no time in taking him hostage, and the Spaniards began plundering the city, the likes of which they had never seen before.

Montezuma's officers and chieftains had no illusions about the mortality of Cortés and his troops, however. These pale men would bleed like any other men, they were certain. Cortés, feeling that the city was securely his as long as he held the Aztec emperor hostage, returned to Veracruz to meet newly arriving Spanish ships. Montezuma was then unceremoniously slain by his own people for his foolishness, and the conquistadores and Tlaxcalans left behind by Cortés to hold the city were attacked. Cortés returned to find his soldiers and the Tlaxcalans engaged in a frantic and disorderly retreat. During the disastrous withdrawal to Tlaxcala, on a rainy and foggy night that became known to the Spaniards as La Noche Triste (the Night of Sorrow), the vengeful Aztec warriors wreaked havoc on the fleeing invaders, killing thousands of Tlaxcalans and more than half of Cortés's men as they tried to make their way back across the causeways. Cortés himself was wounded in the fighting. Many of the retreating Spaniards were weighed down by bags of gold and jewels plundered from the city temples and pyramids. So much for the return of Quetzalcoatl.

Typically, however, Cortés was undaunted. Six months later, with a force of 900 conquistadores and thousands of local Indian allies, the Spaniards assaulted Tenochtitlán. The new Aztec emperor, the courageous Cuauhtémoc, and his army were ready for the attack. A terrible battle ensued, with the Aztecs and the invaders fighting hand to hand throughout Tenochtitlán until the streets and avenues ran with blood and the Spaniards and their allies were forced to retreat. Realizing that he could not take the great city by storm, Cortés and his allies settled in for a siege. Spanish ships blockaded the island city, and for a month and a half the trapped Aztec population slowly starved. They were also wracked by a smallpox epidemic. The disease had arrived from Europe with the invaders, and because the Aztecs, unlike the Europeans, had no natural resistance to it, the smallpox decimated them.

In August 1521, Cortés and his allies launched a final assault. Cuauhtémoc and his army put up a heroic resistance, but in the end they were cornered in the area of Tlatelolco, just north of the great plaza of the main city. There, Cuauhtémoc and his warriors made their final stand, and the final stand of the Aztec empire. They were hacked down and trampled by the ferocious mounted charges of the Spaniards. Cuauhtémoc was captured and executed. It was the end of the Aztec empire, and, in the eyes of Mexicans, the first defeat in a series of defeats at the hands of invading armies.

A new age had indeed begun. The Aztecs were enslaved and given the task of clearing away the rubble of the destroyed Tenochtitlán. Soon, European-style architecture was being erected atop the foundations of the once-great Aztec metropolis. The same fate that had befallen the Aztecs lay in store for the other indigenous peoples of Mexico. More Spaniards came to Mexico. Spanish eventually replaced Nahuatl and the other native languages. Christian missionaries saw to it that the old "pagan" gods and rituals were superseded by the Christian god and saints and Christian rituals, beliefs, and prayers.

But the attempt by the Spanish to replace the centuries-old indigenous cultures with their own European culture was not altogether successful. Unlike the ethnic cleansing and cultural holocaust that Native Americans endured when Europeans overran the present-day United States, what occurred in Mexico,

A 16th-century Spanish map of Tenochtitlán, the Aztec capital. The great city was a series of islands in Lake Texcoco. Today, the lake has been filled in, and Tenochtitlán has become Mexico City, the world's largest urban center.

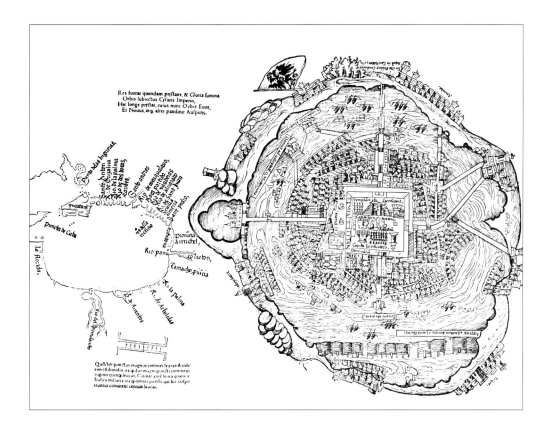

despite the Spaniards' dominance of these lands and
these peoples, was a blending of cultures and peoples,
rather than the wholesale eradication of one in favor
of the other. The most important aspect of this blending was intermarriage between the Spanish and the
native Mexicans. The Spanish married freely among
the Mexicans, and as time passed and mixed-blood
generations were born in Mexico—who in turn married among themselves or married newly arriving
Spaniards or other pure-blood natives—the racial and
cultural distinctions between Spanish and Mexican
became increasingly blurred. A small percentage of
the new population remained purely Spanish, but
by the 1700s, the majority of the Mexican population consisted of a new people—the subjects of both
Cuauhtémoc and Cortés (who fathered what might
have been the first mestizo, a son, by his Aztec mis-
tress); worshipers of the Aztec gods and the Catholic
Trinity; the inhabitants of cities that were a combination of Madrid and Tenochtitlán and of towns that
were a mixture of those found across the Spanish
countryside and those that sprang up on the Mexican
frontier. These people were known as mestizos, and
they in turn gave birth to a new culture, a mixture of
the Old World and the New.

It was a long, troublesome, and chaotic birth for
the new Mexico and the new Mexicans, marred by
convulsions of political anarchy, foreign invasions, revolution, and violence. For a long time, Mexicans suffered from a kind of national identity crisis as they
struggled to come to terms with the bitter origins of
their nation. But with the passage of time, the new
Mexicans endured, and the nation of Mexico developed a distinct culture of its own. On a small church
in present-day Mexico City—a church built atop the
ruins of an Aztec pyramid that stood in what was once
the marketplace of Tlatelolco—there is a plaque. It

reads: "On August 13, 1521, heroically defended by Cuauhtémoc, Tlatelolco fell into the hands of Hernán Cortés. It was neither a triumph nor a defeat: it was the painful birth of the mestizo nation that is Mexico today."

Mexico today is 90 percent mestizo. The old precolonial culture survives in many forms. The fashioning of stunning gold, silver, and turquoise jewelry; the basket weaving and making of colorful woolen ponchos and *frazadas* (blankets); and traditional Indian pottery making are still practiced throughout Mexico by skilled artisans. The national language, however, is Spanish; Roman Catholicism has become deeply rooted among the populace; and European (and now, modern cosmopolitan) architecture is dominant, although the original colonial structures built after the conquest retain certain precolonial aspects because they were constructed primarily by Indian workers. As Mexico became part of the modern world community—however reluctantly at times—mestizo culture was influenced by other sources. Mestizo painting, literature, and music were subject to periodic influxes of artistic movements from abroad, but they always maintained a uniquely mestizo flavor as well. In sports, Mexicans took readily to the Spanish import of bullfighting and equestrian competitions. Later, soccer became the national pastime, and the Mexicans developed a deep affinity for a game that came down from the north—baseball. Another sport that the Mexicans seized upon with unusual fervor originated in England but probably made its way to Mexico via the United States—*el boxeo,* or boxing.

A group of shanties in the slums of Tijuana, Mexico. Like most prizefighters, Julio César Chávez grew up in poverty—unlike other wealthy champions, though, he has chosen to remain in his old neighborhood.

"LA SEGURIDAD DE MI FAMILIA"

The town of Culiacán is a hard place to live and an easy place to die. "Mexicans have known only how to die," wrote Samuel Ramos in *Profile of Man and Culture in Mexico* in 1930, and in Culiacán, this statement holds more truth today than it did when it was first written. The dark and harsh realities of Mexican history have made death an integral part of Mexican culture and the mestizo identity. Perhaps the most important of traditional Mexican holidays is El Día de los Muertos—the Day of the Dead—which celebrates death and the dead. In Culiacán, the opium and marijuana export capital of Mexico, every day is El Día de los Muertos.

Writer Gary Smith, who visited Culiacán in 1992 while he was preparing his superb article on Julio César Chávez for the January 1993 issue of *Sports Illustrated,* offered a description of the town:

> In the place where the world's greatest fighter lives, men eat a leg of goat and drink a can of beer for breakfast. They drive with a gun jammed in their pockets and with a cold beer sweating beneath the denim heat of their legs and with a small red crescent of chili powder sprinkled on the backs of their hands to dab upon their tongues between each swallow. From the speakers of their cars thump songs that tangle love and

bullets and longing while their dark eyes sweep from left to right, alert always for enemies. . . . [I]n the morning, three more bodies are fished from the three rivers that run through the place where the world's greatest fighter lives. . . . Death . . . hangs every night like the moon, just waiting, over a land of men brought up to believe that the beer can between their legs and the accelerator beneath their feet are part of what makes them a man; it hangs there, so pale and fat and low you can touch it.

Located near the western foothills of the Sierra Madre Occidental in steamy Sinaloa, the state that runs along the Gulf of California and the Pacific Ocean, Culiacán is the hometown of Julio César Chávez. Despite the substantial wealth he has accumulated during a career in which he has averaged a fight every three months and now earns about $3 million per championship defense (with the price tag for his services rising by the fight), Chávez has never moved away from this raw, dusty, rural-industrial theater of poverty and sudden mayhem—nor does he plan to.

Chávez's attachment to his hometown is one aspect of his life that provides an insight into his personality, which has often been described with words such as "elusive," "inscrutable," and "impenetrable." In truth, Chávez is easy to understand. He is an intelligent man. But he is also a simple man. The things he desires from life are also simple, although they have not been simple to attain in his case. Nevertheless, what has been interpreted as a lack of personality is in reality the inner calm of a person who knows exactly what his mission in life is, and who has accepted it willingly. Chávez has had this knowledge since he was a boy; a boy who was much too young to be burdened with such knowledge. It is simple, this mission, and Chávez himself describes it simply:

"Para asegurar la seguridad de mi familia"—"to assure the security of my family."

Julio César Chávez was born on July 12, 1962, in Ciudad Obregón, but his family soon moved to Culiacán. Julio was the fourth of 10 children. His father, Rodolfo, worked for a railroad company. The 12 Chávezes lived in a converted railroad car that Rodolfo rented from the company. Rodolfo Chávez apparently was a man of considerable physical courage; the people of Culiacán still tell the story of how Rodolfo jumped into the cab of a burning train loaded with petroleum and drove it away from the refinery where it was unloading oil to a deserted section of track, thus preventing an explosion that could have claimed many lives. But the task of assuring the security of his wife, Isabel, and his 10 offspring was too much for him, and he eventually moved away. Somehow teenage Julio, his mother, and his siblings all knew that it would be Julio who would shoulder his father's burden. It was Julio who had the character, even as a boy, to accept this lot. Even then there was something about him—a quiet confidence, a self-assurance, an inner strength—that all the other members of his family, including his mother and older brothers and sisters, looked to. Julio was the one. Julio would make things right.

This capacity—to do what was necessary to succeed, to overcome—would stay with Julio, eventually becoming the dominant aspect of his in-the-ring persona. It would become both a personal philosophy and a part of his inner self. As a teenage boy trying to provide for and nurture a family of 11 in a dirt-poor town where stray machine gun fire occasionally ripped through the windows of his home at night, it was much to ask. But Julio was up before dawn and home after dark, finding whatever work there was to be had—delivering papers, working as a shoemaker's helper, hawking chewing gum on the dusty streets, washing cars, working at a taco stand—taking on any manual labor, however grueling, he could find. At the same time, it was Julio who comforted his mother in her time of need, who consoled his older sisters in the wake of broken love affairs or the sudden, violent death of some handsome, gun-toting, hot-tempered lover, and who kept an eye on all his brothers and sisters in a place where trouble found you rather than the other way around.

Inevitably, Julio could only do so much. One hot Culiacán night, his four-year-old brother, Omar, was hit and killed by a drunk driver. Julio ran to the hospital and arrived in time to watch his brother die from the injuries. After that, Julio changed. A certain happiness and laughter that had always played in his eyes was no longer there. The choir-boy handsomeness and the astonishingly bright and boyish smile that occasionally lit up his features and attracted the covetous glances of every beautiful, dark-eyed señorita over the age of 13 in Culiacán (Sinaloa is famous for its

Children play around a polluted pond in a Mexico City slum. Like many youngsters from impoverished Mexican families, Chávez was forced to become a man long before his time: as a teenager he not only worked from dawn to dusk to bring in money but also had to protect his nine brothers and sisters in the often violent environment of Culiacán.

beautiful women) remained, but the smile did not appear so often anymore, and the angelic face now held an expression of care and worry, and, when Julio thought no one was watching, of profound loss and grief. Julio never got over Omar's death; the tragedy haunts him still. Even now, with so much time passed, with so much changed in his and his family's life, Chávez still mourns for his lost brother. To this day, when he visits his brother's gravesite, the greatest and "toughest, bar none" prizefighter in the world weeps openly. The passage of time proved that Julio César Chávez could do everything and anything for his family—except to bring back Omar. Perhaps that is one of the primary reasons why Chávez has never left Culiacán and swears he will stay there "todos mis días"—"all of my days." His family—a large extended group that includes his wife, Amalia, and three children, as well as in-laws, cousins, aunts and uncles, numerous *compañeros,* and his trainers—is in Culiacán, but Chávez now has enough money to take them all with him if he relocated. But Omar is there also, in the very earth of Culiacán, and Julio cannot take Omar. Julio will never leave his *hermano pequeño* behind. He was not near him to protect him—to assure his security—on that hot, dark night so many years ago, as he no doubt felt and still feels he should have been; but he will now stay near him always.

When Julio was 16, two of his older brothers, Rodolfo and Rafael, concluded that there might be a way Julio could earn some decent money. They had noticed what happened when Julio got involved in street fights with other young, tough hombres in their town. Such fights were inevitable in a place like Culiacán—fights over girls, jobs, or insults; adolescent displays of traditional Mexican machismo; and fights for their own sake—for in Mexico, boxing is as popular as, for example, baseball is in the United States, and children and teenagers will square off and box one another with no more reservation than a bunch of youngsters in Ohio would have choosing up sides for a ballgame on a local field.

When Julio fought, Rodolfo and Rafael noticed two things, primarily. The first was that when Julio's adversaries hit Julio—and they usually hit him first— no matter how big and strong they might be, nothing happened. It was as if they had punched a brick wall. The second was that when Julio hit them back, once, maybe twice, the fight was over. If he hit them in the head, they ended up sprawled in the dust. If he hit them in the stomach, or chest, or even in the shoulder, they quickly decided that they did not want to fight anymore.

Rodolfo and Rafael, who had done some boxing themselves, persuaded Julio to give it a try. Julio was an excellent athlete. He had strong legs and shoulders. He was not a fast runner, but he was nimble with his feet and inexhaustible, qualities he displayed whenever he had a chance to play soccer, his favorite sport, or baseball. Julio reacted reluctantly at first to his brothers' proposal. But when they told him he might be able to bring home some relatively significant money for the household, he agreed. And once he agreed to the idea, he characteristically dedicated himself to it with a workmanlike and relentless single-mindedness. With his brothers acting as trainers and managers, he prepared himself to box. Then he began fighting locally. He had a small number of amateur fights to hone his skills, then he turned professional—there was no money to be had in amateur boxing—fighting as a super featherweight at about 130 pounds.

Chávez's first professional opponents were other boxers from Culiacán or nearby towns. The fights were held on dusty ranches outside of town. Dogs, chickens, and other livestock occasionally inter-

Chávez mourns at the grave of his brother Omar, killed at the age of four by a drunk driver. During the Chávez family's 1993 visit to the Culiacán cemetery, the unbeaten champion broke down in tears, lamenting, "Now I am rich and famous and I have everything, but I still don't have you."

rupted the proceedings, which resembled cockfights more than anything else, with hard-looking men passing bottles of tequila and wagering on the outcome. Chávez's first professional fight was on February 5, 1980, in Culiacán, against Andrés Félix. Chávez knocked Félix out in the first round. Chávez fought nine more bouts that year, winning them all by knockout or technical knockout. Word started getting around about the son of Rodolfo Chávez. The grizzled men would nod knowingly as Julio walked away from each fight, leaving yet another young man sitting dazed and bleeding among the clucking chickens after a brief exchange of punches. They all started betting their *dinero* on the Chávez kid. Julio took the first decent purse he earned from a match and bought his mother a washing machine.

CHAPULTEPEC

The Mexico in which Julio Céser Chávez grew to manhood had begun to establish its identity by the 19th century. A new Mexican nationalism was taking root, allowing Mexicans to take pride in being Mexicans. Unfortunately, the events that followed would deeply scar Mexico's cultural and national self-image. The scars remain to this day.

The deepest of these scars—more like the loss of a limb than a mere scar—was inflicted in 1946–47 by Mexico's rapidly growing neighbor to the north. The United States, afflicted with an expansionist fever that was justified by a philosophy known by the grandiose term *Manifest Destiny*—which, loosely translated, meant "let's grab all the territory we can while we can, regardless of who it actually belongs to"—was acting the part of continental and international bully. Unconsciously, or perhaps consciously, the young America was behaving much like Great Britan, the nation they had so recently wrested independence from. Manifest Destiny was, in fact, the urge to establish an ocean-to-ocean empire; and had not the Civil War interrupted things, there is no telling when or where this runaway Napoleonism might have ended.

In 1845, newly elected president James K. Polk set about the task of realizing his nation's "destiny." He annexed the territory of Texas and then set his sights on the northern expanses of Mexican territory that

General Zachary Taylor, one of the commanders of the U.S. forces in the Mexican War of 1846–47. Mexico's defeat in the war and the loss of nearly half its territory—the present-day American Southwest—dealt a devastating blow to the nation's self-esteem.

are known today as the American Southwest. After a
token offer to buy this territory from Mexico, which
was summarily refused, Polk decided to take it. He
placed American troops near the border along the Rio
Grande in order to provoke a confrontation with
Mexican troops patrolling their side of the border.
Inevitably, the large concentration of American soldiers (3,000 troops under the command of General
Zachary Taylor) moving along the border had the
desired provocative effect, and a confrontation ensued.
Shots were fired. This was the excuse the Polk admin-
istration was looking for, and Congress lost no time in
declaring war on Mexico and launching an invasion.
Among the soldiers who took part in the invasion of
Mexico was a young quartermaster from Ohio named
Ulysses S. Grant. Grant aptly summed up the blatant,
cynical provocation and the war that followed, calling
it "one of the most unjust ever waged by a stronger
against a weaker nation. It was an instance of a repub-
lic following the bad example of European monar-
chies in not considering justice in their desire to
acquire additional territories."

Polk had no such qualms. An invasion force led by
General Winfield Scott landed at Veracruz and began
a hell-bent march on Mexico City. As if to unnerve
the Mexicans by reminding them of a previous invasion that had changed their nation forever, Scott's
army followed the same route inland toward Mexico
City that Cortés and his conquistadores had taken
three centuries before on their march to Tenochtitlán.
The Mexicans put up a fierce resistance as the Americans drove inland, and pitched battles were fought at
Cerro Gordo, Contreras, Churubusco, and Molino del
Rey. But the invaders' advance could not be stopped,
and the Mexicans were forced to give ground again
and again. A final, bitter confrontation occurred at the
ancient, heavily fortified citadel of Chapultepec—the

final obstacle standing between the Americans and Mexico City itself.

The Battle of Chapultepec, fought on September 8, 1847, was ferocious and tragic. As the Americans finally gained the upper hand, many of the defenders of the citadel, most of whom were barely teenagers (Mexican president and general Antonio López de Santa Anna had pulled his seasoned regulars back within the city), committed suicide in a final act of defiance by hurling themselves down from the high cliffs into the midst of the invading troops. According to legend, some of these young Mexican kamikazes wrapped themselves in Mexican flags before leaping.

Having taken Chapultepec after a final sequence of bloody hand-to-hand combat with its remaining defenders, the American troops assaulted Mexico City. The Mexican army put up a brief resistance, but Santa Anna, playing the part of a latter-day Montezuma, withdrew from the city with his entire army during the night, abandoning the pride of Mexico to the invaders. The capital city of Mexico was left in the hands of the Americans. A harsh treaty was then imposed on Mexico, in which the

Zachary Taylor, known as Old Rough and Ready, commanding his troops at the Battle of Buena Vista in February 1847. Despite the bravery and superior numbers of the Mexican army, Taylor's forces won a decisive victory at Buena Vista. His success on the battlefield led to his election as president of the United States in 1848.

gigantic expanse of territory that is now California, New Mexico, Utah, Nevada, Arizona, and Colorado—about one-half of Mexico in 1847—was ceded to the United States.

The Mexican War (as it is known in the United States) was the most deeply humiliating occurrence in Mexican history. A vastly outnumbered army of invaders had marched into their nation, forced the Mexican army to retreat again and again, and had then taken their capital city. The leader of the Mexican troops had retreated in the night rather than defend Mexico City. And when the invaders left, they took with them a huge parcel of Mexican territory. Although Mexicans seized on what little positive aspects of the event they could—most Mexican towns and cities, for example, now have streets named after or monuments honoring Los Hijo Martires de Chapultepec (The Child Martyrs of Chapultepec)—the bitter facts of the retreat, the abandonment of Mexico City, and the loss of territory could not, and to this day cannot, be ignored or forgotten. As Alan Riding writes in his study of Mexico and Mexicans, *Distant Neighbors,* "The past remains alive in the Mexican soul."

Mexicans take their history seriously. Mexicans also take their boxing seriously. Their boxers represent Mexican athleticism and the traditional Mexican qualities of machismo in their purest form. Mexican pugilists start young, train religiously, and learn a hard, uncompromising style of fighting. Mexican prizefighters come to the ring to work; to hit their opponent hard and to continue hitting him hard until he is broken. Endurance, the ability to absorb punishment, the art of "cutting off the ring" (neutralizing a mobile opponent's maneuvering space and blocking his avenues of escape by moving in certain angles in response to the opponent's movement), setting one's legs to achieve maximum punching leverage, hard counterpunching, and the subtle nuances of defense during toe-to-toe infighting are emphasized. Body punching is stressed from the beginning. In the United States, the left jab to the face is considered the fundamental punch, the blow that sets up all other blows and that must be established to control a fight. In Mexico, it is the hook to the body (the *hard* hook to the body) that is considered the fundamental punch.

The primary feature of a contest between two Mexican pugilists is what might be termed the territorial imperative. Alan Riding writes of Mexico that "in few countries in the world [is] history . . . so mirrored in—and a mirror of—the character of its people." Historically, the loss of territory as the result of retreat and a refusal or inability to stand one's ground in the face of a hostile advance, especially in relation to the Mexican War, is a shameful burden carried by the Mexican national persona. Culturally, Mexicans have been reacting to this and other foreign incursions into their territory ever since. Sociologists and boxing analysts have always recognized that the boxing ring is much more than a mere "sports arena"; that it is often the focus of, and an outlet for, cultural tensions, a metaphor of larger national and international cultural and political events and trends.

It is no surprise, then, that in a nation historically victimized by invasion and humiliated by retreat and a subsequent loss of national pride and territory; a nation where "the past remains alive" and "history is mirrored in the character of its people"; the primary metaphor and ritual drama played out by Mexican boxers is one of territoriality. Mexican fighters are acutely aware of the ring as territory. They strive to take it and control it, and despair at the thought of backing up, or giving ground. A fight between two Mexican boxers begins in center ring and often develops into a succession of linear movements backward

A 19th-century engraving shows Mexican commander Antonio López de Santa Anna fleeing from the Battle of Cerro Gordo on April 18, 1847. Santa Anna's poor generalship throughout the war was largely responsible for the victory of the invading U.S. troops.

and forward with the two fighters locked closely together in toe-to-toe infighting. It is a series of straight-ahead offensives and counteroffensives, during which leg and upper-body strength, the ability to give and take a punch, inside defensive technique, and sheer will are tested.

From 1981 to 1983, the young Julio César Chávez claimed quite a bit of territory as he fought his way through the brutal, gladitorial phase of Mexico's professional prizefighting world. There are 77 million people in Mexico. Each year, every town and city produces a host of young men who hope to one day follow in the footsteps of the honored and legendary Mexican champions of the past and present. Beginning in 1944 with Juan Zurita of Guadalajara, there have been to date 70 (and counting) Mexican world champions; Mexico has produced more world champions than any other nation except the United States. Among the most honored of Mexico's pugilists are the unparalleled and deeply lamented Salvador Sánchez (Sánchez was killed at the age of 23 in a car accident; he was already world featherweight champion and was so naturally gifted that there is no telling what heights he might have achieved had he lived), Lupe

Pintor, Pipino Cuevas, Lauro Salas, Rodrigo González, Carlos Zarate, Carlos Palomino, Rubén Oliveras—the list goes on. In order to achieve such status, or even a chance at a title fight, up-and-coming Mexican fighters must endure a brutal process of elimination, fighting their way past opposition that is tough to start with and grows tougher as a boxer graduates from regional contests and begins to face fighters from all parts of Mexico.

Given the cultural, historical, and stylistic aspects of Mexican prizefighting, add the need and the will of young, tough Mexican men who see boxing as their only avenue of escape from a life of poverty and hard labor, throw in the ever-present machismo factor, and it becomes clear that Chávez had a hard march in those first years. In effect, he was fighting, on a monthly and even bimonthly schedule, the pugilistic equivalents of the Child Martyrs of Chapultepec—young, desperate combatants who refused to back up. He himself was one of them. Not surprisingly, these fights usually did not last long. Chávez's chin, body, and fists were as hard as the packed earth surrounding high Chapultepec, and when his opponents hurled themselves against them, the opponents were quickly broken. From the older, more seasoned veterans that Chávez faced during his march toward a title shot, he learned the rougher aspects of the trade—how to use the thumb of the glove to close an opponent's eye; how to twist a glove on impact in order to open a cut on an opponent's face; how to use the raised seams or laces of the gloves to reopen cuts; how to use knees, elbows, forearms, and shoulders to keep an opponent pinned in a corner and to batter the opponent's entire body; how to pull an opponent's head forward with one hand while delivering a punch with the other. Having learned such lessons for a few rounds, Chávez would then knock out the instructor.

In 1981–82, Chávez fought 23 bouts. He knocked out 22 of his opponents. Only five of them lasted past the fifth round. Eddy Acosta, Victor Gómez, Miguel Ruiz, Jesús Lara, Fidel Navarro, Bobby Domínguez, Daniele Martínez, Sonny Boy Ramírez, Ramón Luque, Jesús García, Indio Peraza, Ernesto Herra, and Gustavo Salgado were all dispatched in round 1 or 2. Managers and promoters began to take notice of this baby-faced kid from Culiacán. They saw a fighter with knockout power in both hands, a devastating body attack, an assortment of punches that were thrown with an uncanny precision and accuracy, an iron chin, and an imperturbable concentration in the ring. He seemed relaxed and in complete command of the proceedings no matter what was going on during a bout—and usually, at this point, the bouts were toe-to-toe slug-fests. The expression on his face rarely changed. Each fight was like another day at the office. Chávez climbed into the ring, did what he had to do, and went home. In so doing, he left a trail of pulverized opponents from Culiacán to Tijuana and back. Félix Ramón, a veteran manager of Mexican fighters, saw a boxer with something special. Chávez, he believed, was a "can't miss" prospect, and soon he had signed a contract to manage the young boxer's career.

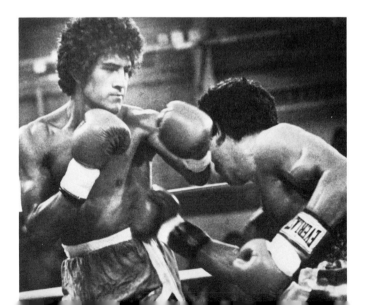

Featherweight champion Salvador Sánchez (left) was one of the great representatives of the proud Mexican boxing tradition. When the 23-year-old Sánchez died in a March 1982 automobile accident, he had barely begun to realize his potential in the ring.

Ramón began to steer the newest member of his stable of fighters toward a title shot. Chávez began fighting in larger arenas against increasingly tougher and better-known opponents. He destroyed them, went home, bought things for his friends and family, and trained until his next fight. His bouts began to receive coverage on Mexican television. But although he was making a name for himself in Mexico, he was still unheard of in the United States or in Central and South American boxing circles at large. Ramón knew that in order to garner the publicity his fighter needed for a title shot and the big money that might follow, Chávez needed television coverage in the United States. Ramón went to work across the border and set up a fight in Los Angeles at the Olympic Auditorium on June 15, 1983, between Chávez and Romero Sandoval of Los Angeles. The fight would be on the undercard of a heavyweight matchup, but Sandoval was a well-known and popular boxer in the area and was sure to draw an early crowd. Most important, the bout would receive some local television coverage in the United States.

Chávez was determined to make the most of this opportunity. Sandoval was a tough and experienced fighter who had battled some of the best men in the division. Chávez walked through Sandoval's punches and in round 3 destroyed him with a coldly deliberate violence that initially stunned the small crowd of Sandoval supporters who had come to see the pre-liminary bouts. But as Chávez prepared to leave the ring, they stood and cheered. The television announcers had commented that despite his gaudy record coming into the bout—34 wins with 33 knockouts—Chávez was unranked by any of the three governing bodies. This situation now changed quickly, just as Ramón had hoped. Chávez fought six more contests, against ranked opponents. He knocked them all out.

"WHY WOULD I WANT A REMATCH?"

Chávez demonstrates his form for a group of local fans during a California training session. Chávez's third fight in the United States, a spectacular, bloody war with fellow Mexican Mario Martínez in September 1984, ended in an eighth-round technical knockout of Martínez and earned Chávez the WBC super-featherweight championship.

While Mexico was in the process of forging a cultural identity, it was also attempting to establish a political one. This process plunged the nation into a convulsive century of anarchy and mayhem. Mexico's inner torment had already begun by the time General Winfield Scott led his victorious army into the Zócalo in 1847. The initial conflicts were centered around Mexico's attempts to achieve independence from Spain. In September 1810, 57-year-old Padre Miguel Hidalgo y Costilla, a rural parish priest, aided by the subversive Captain Ignacio Allende, led a bedraggled army of some 20,000 impoverished and downtrodden Indians and mestizos in an attempt to overthrow the Spanish imperial government that had ruled Mexico since the victory of Cortés over the Aztec Empire. Bristling with machetes, axes, knives, and agricultural tools, and following the banner of the Virgin of Guadalupe (the image of the Virgin Mary that appeared to a humble Indian in 1531), this barefoot band of revolutionaries hacked and burned its way toward Mexico City before it was finally defeated by Spanish troops at Guadalajara. Both Allende and Hidalgo were captured and executed. Hidalgo was put to death by firing squad and then beheaded, after which his unfortunate and frowning head was put on display for 10 years at the Spanish garrison in Guanajuato, whose occupants had been massacred by the revolutionaries during their abortive march on Mexico City.

Allende and Hidalgo were but the first in a long line of Mexican revolutionary *hombres de la gente* (men of the people) who would eventually find themselves on the wrong end of a rope or a firing squad or an assassin's knife or pistol. Padre José María Morelos, another village priest, attempted to continue Hidalgo's rebellion. He was captured and executed in 1815. In 1821, another revolutionary army, led by the ruthless and equally courageous Colonel Agustín de Iturbide and one of the last surviving rebels of the earlier uprisings, Vicente Guerrero, succeeded in ousting the Spanish once and for all. On July 21, 1822, Iturbide was crowned Emperor Agustín I; by December, mutinies and uprisings by Mexican army factions had driven him from the country. (Iturbide returned in 1824 and was quickly executed.)

The ensuing political anarchy that plagued the newly independent Mexico was of such cartoonish proportions that it would have been comic had it not been for the bloodshed and suffering it engendered. Historians have long been aware that civil wars are often the most brutal and vindictive of affairs, and Mexico was no exception. When Mexicans fight Mexicans, in the prizefighting ring or on the battlefield, no quarter is asked and none is given. Perhaps, in brutalizing themselves in the manner witnessed throughout the 19th and early 20th centuries, Mexicans were venting on one another the hostility and vengefulness they felt toward those foreign invaders who had brutalized them.

The seemingly endless cycle of uprising, vicious reprisal, brutal suppression, and new uprising pitted a bewildering variety of political factions, armies, leaders, heroes, and villains against one another in the name of an equally bewildering variety of political and social movements and causes, but the basic adversarial foundation of the unrest was simple—the "haves" versus the "have nots." As Quartermaster Ulysses S. Grant noted during his stay in Mexico following the U.S. invasion, Mexico was a nation where "the rich keep down the poor with a hardness of heart that is incredible."

Republicans, Monarchists, Constitutional Monarchists, Liberals, Conservatives, Reelectionists, Antireelectionists, and even a faction known as Scientists, vied for Spanish, European, North American, military, and popular support, while the Mexican government changed hands no less than 50 times between 1820 and 1884. Revolutions, rebellions, uprisings, caste wars, and coups d'état followed one after another. And always, the true Mexican heroes, the hombres de la gente, appeared to bring periods of hope to the oppressed, the disenfranchised, the persecuted and impoverished masses of mestizos and Indians. Just as inevitably, they were imprisoned, murdered, or forced to flee their nation, dying in exile in foreign lands. It seemed that Mexican heroes were born to die.

It is surprising that neither of the two young Mexican combatants who climbed into the ring at the Los Angeles Forum on September 13, 1984, joined the long list of Mexican martyrs, considering the events that took place between them that evening. Both boxers were known as knockout artists; between the two of them, they had dispatched 66 opponents—a startling statistic, considering the fact that Chávez was only 23 and Mario Martínez, of Guadalajara, was a mere 19 years of age. Nor could there be found two less likely looking ring assassins. Chávez still looked as if he should have been singing in a boys' choir, and the handsome Martínez, with his unruly crop of tousled black hair, a Zapataesque mustache, and black, classically melancholy Mexican eyes, presented an equally appealing figure. Before they were even called to the center of the ring, the two young Mexicans saluted one another amiably from their corners.

In prizefighting, however, appearances can be deceiving, and the respective records of the two fighters indicated that this championship bout would not be decided by the judges' scorecards. Chávez was 41-0, with 37 knockouts, and Martinez was 28-1, with 26 knockouts. And yet, despite their records, nobody, except perhaps the two pugilists themselves, could have been prepared for the nonstop, eight-round explosion of violence that occurred in the ring that night. During his long career, which so far has spanned 13 years, 88 fights, and 26 championship bouts, many of them against some of the roughest, toughest fighters in four different weight divisions, Julio César Chávez has fought a good number of brutal "no-quarter" contests. None of them, however, have matched in sheer, unrelenting ferocity the pitched battle he was about to wage with Mario Martínez of Guadalajara.

The bout began in the conventional manner, with the two boxers circling one another warily in the center of the ring, exchanging tentative jabs in the customary "feeling-out" process. With 40 seconds remaining in the first round, all hell broke loose. The two fighters came together shoulder to shoulder, forehead to forehead. Martínez, displaying bull-like strength, muscled Chávez backward until Chávez was on the ropes. The young man from Guadalajara then attempted to decapitate his opponent, launching a profusion of bombs with both fists. They came in one after another, wide, looping "haymakers" aimed at Chávez's head. There was no attempt at pugilistic subtlety here; Martínez wound up and threw his punches like some kind of ambidextrous, side-armed fastball pitcher.

Chávez, naturally, began ducking. Martínez tele-graphed his bombardment in such a blatant manner that everyone in the arena could see when and from where the punches were coming, but they came in such numbers and with so little time between them that some of them invariably got through. Chávez, for his part, answered each missed punch, and each one that landed, for that matter, with short, jarring upper-cuts and hooks to Martínez's jaw. The punches, from both fighters, flew with ever-increasing force and in ever-increasing numbers. When the bell rang to end the round, the crowd was on its feet, roaring. The two fighters stepped back and nodded respectfully to each other before returning to their corners.

Rounds 2 and 3 were identical to the first, with Chávez's back to the ropes and Martínez right on top of him. For the remainder of the fight, except for brief intervals, no more than three or four inches would separate the two boxers. Neither fighter had slowed

Chávez's punching style is comparable to that of the legendary heavy-weight champion Joe Louis, shown here during his 1936 bout with Max Schmeling. Like Louis, Chávez throws short, accurate, devastating punches in a variety of combinations.

down; if anything there were more punches thrown
with more force behind them. But a pattern that did
not bode well for Martínez was beginning to emerge.
Chávez's short, direct punches traveled in a straight
line to their target, while Martínez's blows were wide
swings that looped outward and then inward. Chávez
thus began landing combinations of two or three
punches—to the midsection, jaw, face, and head—in
the intervals between incoming blows. And because
Martínez telegraphed his blows, Chávez could slip
and duck many of them. Each time Martínez missed,
Chávez punished him with pistonlike counterpunches as
Martínez recoiled and set himself to launch another
volley. And Chávez did not miss. Much like the heavyweight Joe Louis, who could destroy an opponent
with blows that traveled a mere six inches or so, the
punches of Chávez were short and accurate; they shot
out directly from the defensive position in which he
held his gloves, with no windup to alert Martínez as
to whether a left or right was coming, and they landed
with a jarring force again and again. Martínez did not
care. He fired away regardless.

Round 4: Martínez bulled Chávez onto the ropes
and bombed away tirelessly, missing with some
punches and landing others with terrific force.
Chávez hacked and chopped with a brutal precision in return. The pace and ferocity escalated each
time one fighter stunned the other, for the stunned
fighter would immediately retaliate in order to
show his opponent that he was *not* stunned. The
round ended with Martínez and Chávez engaged in
a fierce blow-for-blow exchange that continued
after the bell rang and did not stop until the referee,
a courageous man indeed, inserted himself into the
maelstrom and pried the boxers apart. The crowd
still had not retaken their seats, nor would they for
the duration of the contest.

Something had to give. A boxing match depends on psychological factors as much as physical considerations, and in round 5, Chávez established a psychological edge. The moment came early in the round. Martínez advanced on Chávez at the bell. Chávez backed up to the ropes, and as Martínez came within range, Chávez nailed him with a terrific right to the head. Martínez, rattled, backed off. Chávez remained on the ropes and beckoned with his gloves for Martínez to join him again. Martínez obliged, throwing a big right as he came, but before it could reach its target, Chávez jolted Martínez with a left-right combination of uppercuts to the jaw. Martínez attempted to tie up his opponent's arms, whereupon Chávez executed a classic boxing maneuver, trapping the right arm of Martínez under his own left armpit and turning Martínez around so that *his* back was against the ropes. Chávez then unloaded on Martínez with digging punches to the body and head. Martínez attempted to escape by sliding to his right along the ropes. Chávez remained in front of Martínez, moving along parallel with him; Martínez thus moved only laterally and subsequently found himself in the corner. Trapped there, he received a shellacking from Chávez, who would not allow Martínez to escape the cul-de-sac. True to form, Martínez simply let loose with his own volley, finally managing to free himself and land some hard punches of his own before the bell rang to end the round.

When he came out for round 6, however, Martínez was showing clear signs of attrition. He could no longer force Chávez against the ropes, and now Martínez began to find himself backed up and pinned on the ropes. His punches were fewer and it took him longer to launch them. Chávez, in the meantime, stepped up his attack, pounding Martínez to the body and landing violent blows to his opponent's face. He picked his spots, driving in his punches below, between, and over the punches of Martínez. By the time the round ended, Martínez's eyes were swelling and he was bleeding from the mouth and nose. Nevertheless, he was throwing—and landing—hard punches when the bell to end the round sounded. The Mexican television commentator remarked on the "enorme corazón" (enormous heart) of the fighter from Guadalajara as he returned to his corner.

The final two rounds were brutal. Martínez, sensing that he was losing the fight, launched desperate attacks in each round. He rocked Chávez on several occasions, but Chávez was now relentless, and he assaulted Martínez's face with chopping, ruthlessly accurate combinations. As round 8 drew to a close, Martínez's face was, as the commentator put it, "una máscara de sangre"—"a mask of blood." The crowd was screaming for the referee to stop the contest. Martínez was on the verge of going down when the round ended, and his blood sprayed about the ring with each punch Chávez landed. Remarkably, however, when the bell sounded to end the round, Martínez was still throwing punches. As he unsteadily made his way back to his corner, the referee signaled that the war was over. Julio César Chávez was declared winner by technical knockout and new WBC superfeatherweight champion. His cornermen, including his brothers Rodolfo and Rafael, hoisted the new *campeón* on their shoulders. Martínez slumped into a chair in his own corner as his trainer and the other cornermen attended to him, covering his face with towels. When they removed them, much of the blood was wiped away. Although his face was swollen and lacerated, 19-year-old Mario Martínez's dark eyes were clear. They registered a bitter disappointment, and a sadness that he clearly felt to the depths of his soul.

Though much admired by the public, brawler Jack Dempsey (left) defended his heavyweight title only three times between 1919 and 1926 and refused to fight black contenders. He was dethroned in 1926 by the superb boxer Gene Tunney (right). By contrast, Julio César Chávez has averaged five bouts a year since capturing his first championship in 1984.

In professional prizefighting, there are two kinds of champions. There are what are known in boxing circles as fighting champions, and then there are the other kind. Fighting champions defend their title regularly, taking on the top contenders as well as lesser-ranked fighters without long intervals of inactivity between bouts. The other type fight sporadically, carefully picking and choosing their opponents, and only making mandatory title defenses as decreed by the governing body they fight under. Joe Louis (25 title defenses), Henry Armstrong and Eusebio Pedroza (20 title defenses each), and the Thai junior-bantamweight legend Khaosai Galaxy (19 title defenses, 19 knockouts) are at the top of the list of fighting champions. Jack Dempsey was a member of the nonfighting ilk—while heavyweight champion, he twice allowed intervals of two years to pass before he stepped back into the ring, and his manager picked his opponents with great care (that is, until they signed to fight Gene Tunney, who, as a light-heavyweight making the jump to the heavyweight class, seemed like easy game). Recently, Riddick Bowe was essentially a nonfighter—after wresting the heavyweight title from Evander Holyfield in an inspired contest, he defended it with extreme care, fighting rarely and against pathetic competition handpicked by his manager, Rock Newman. Mike Tyson, by contrast, was a fighting champion during the early part of his career, accomplishing the ultimate task in today's boxing world—unifying a weight division title by defeating the champions of the three different governing bodies. Even in the midst of the spectacular personal crash-and-burn downslide that eventually landed him in prison as a convicted rapist, Tyson attempted to fight as regularly as possible.

Regrettably, true fighting champions are for the most part a thing of the past; in the United States especially, they seem to be a vanishing breed. Most of today's champions, especially in the upper weight classes, are content to rest on their laurels, and once a year or so fight a tune-up against an easy opponent followed by a big-money title bout against a name contender. Significantly, one of the most active heavyweights in recent years has been George Foreman, a graduate of the Muhammad Ali–Joe Frazier–Ken Norton school of fighting heavyweights. Foreman, well over 40 years of age, managed the difficult task of keeping his massive body in fighting trim—perhaps fighting "shape" would be a better word for Big George, as the name George Foreman and the word *trim* constitute something of an oxymoron—by fighting as frequently as possible during the early years of his comeback. Granted, Big George fought his share of stiffs, but he fought. (Foreman's record currently stands at 76 wins and 4 losses, with 67 knockouts.)

Joe Louis was unfairly criticized for the occasionally less-than-prime-quality competition he faced as champion. "He did it for the money," was the usual complaint. This is in part true; but in Louis's day, even champions of his caliber—Louis is considered by many to be the best heavyweight in prizefighting history—were not making the megabucks today's heavyweight champs can earn even in a nontitle fight. But there is more to it than that. Louis felt a responsibility to his fans and supporters to give them the opportunity to see him ply his trade as frequently as possible. And there simply were not many heavyweights around who were in the same echelon as Louis. Louis beat the legitimate contenders, gave them rematches, and beat them again, and while he waited for new contenders to appear, he fought the next-best thing. Furthermore, as the best boxing trainers are fond of saying, "there is no substitute for a real fight in the ring"; meaning that no matter how much a boxer may train and spar, the best way to stay in fighting shape is to fight, even against lesser opponents. This is one of the secrets behind the long-term success of fighters of the past, such as Louis, Willie Pep, and the ageless ring wizard Archie Moore (who fought 220 bouts). Contemporary fighting champions who have maintained long and productive careers, include the great middleweight Marvin Hagler; the remarkable featherweight and then junior-lightweight champion Azumah Nelson of Ghana (at age 35, Nelson has become a latter-day, pocket-sized Archie Moore); and Rocky Lockridge. Because they maintained or maintain a rigorous fighting schedule throughout their careers, they avoided or avoid acquiring "ring rust"— the inevitable corrosion of reflexes, stamina, and general ring skills—that bedevils even young fighters who take long layoffs between matches. And, finally, there are those pugilists who are *warriors* in the truest sense of the word. They do not wear the label *fighter* lightly. They live it. They are fighters, and so they fight. These are the best of them.

There is a downside to acting the part of a fighting champion. Some fighters—especially those whose boxing style requires them to take a lot of punishment in a bout—may burn out quickly from the cumulative effects of their frequent activity. Or, as was the case with Muhammad Ali, they may simply not know when to quit, which can have disastrous consequences. And there is always the chance that on some off night, a champion might lose his title to an inferior fighter. After all, the more one fights, the greater the chances that on some given night, for some reason or combination of reasons, one may be beaten. The most famous example of this phenomenon occurred when the apparently indestructible heavyweight terror Mike Tyson lost his title to a doughboy named Buster Douglas in Tokyo on February 11, 1990. The official odds against Douglas, a professional nobody who resembled a pugilistic Michelin Man, beating Tyson were something like 50 to 1. But Douglas, apparently possessed by the spirit of Sonny Liston that night, gave

In choosing to fight with a regularity that is rare among today's prizefighters, Chávez has followed the example of such legendary ring warriors as Archie Moore (left), who captured the light-heavyweight crown from Joey Maxim (right) in December 1952. One of the all-time great ring artists, the ageless Moore fought 220 bouts over a 20-year career and still holds the record for career knockouts with 127.

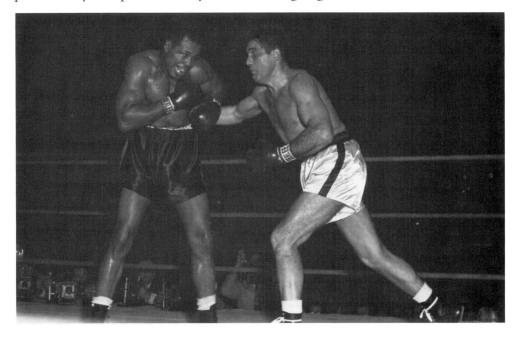

Tyson the beating of his life and knocked him out in the 10th round, shocking the sports world and becoming the new heavyweight champion. Douglas was *not* a fighting champion. In his first title defense, he was decked by Evander Holyfield in the second round. In the Tyson bout, Douglas had easily gotten to his feet after being sent to the canvas by what was then the most fearsome punch to be found anywhere in boxing—a Mike Tyson right uppercut. And Douglas was clearly in command of his senses after his knockdown by Holyfield, who was a light-heavyweight attempting to make the jump to the heavies, and who subsequently, although he possessed tireless stamina and a lion's heart, did not possess a heavyweight's punching power. Nevertheless, Douglas decided to remain on the canvas for the 10 count. He then took the $15 million or so he "earned" for the bout, returned to his hometown of Columbus, Ohio, built himself a mansion with a number of televisions in each room, and became the ultimate couch potato, quickly ballooning to 350 pounds.

Julio César Chávez is a fighting champion. He is a *fighter*—a throwback to the former ring gladiators such as Jimmy Wilde, Willie Pep, Benny Leonard, Sandy Sadler, Henry Armstrong, and Sugar Ray Robinson. From April 19, 1985, to August 21, 1987, he fought 12 bouts, averaging a fight every three months—an unheard-of pace for a champion in contemporary prizefighting. Nine of the 12 fights were title defenses against some of the toughest, most talented fighters in a division that, at the time, sported a wealth of formidable pugilists, including Dwight Pratchett, Refugio Rojas, Rubén Castillo, Roger Mayweather, Rocky Lockridge, and Juan LaPorte.

Chávez did not wait long to serve notice to the other super-featherweight contenders that they had a wolf in their midst. Less than three months after winning the championship, Chávez annihilated Manny Hernández in three rounds in a nontitle fight in Mexico City. Three and a half months later, on April 19, 1985, he made his first title defense, against Rubén Castillo in Los Angeles. The 27-year-old Mexican-American Castillo was a veteran of 67 bouts. Castillo was a warrior. His record of 64 wins, 4 losses, and 2 draws included bouts against some of the best fighters to pound their way through the lighter weight ranks since the mid-1970s. Castillo was a perennial contender, having fought for a championship four times. In those bouts, he was beaten by three boxing legends—Alexis Arguëllo, Salvador Sánchez, and Azumah Nelson—and had come within one point on a judge's scorecard of taking the title from the superb Juan LaPorte.

Castillo, who had once again battled his way back to becoming the WBC's number one ranked contender, was sure that in fighting Chávez, he would finally realize his long-sought dream of a championship belt. All the sweat and blood and pain of 70 professional prizefights would finally pay off. All the experience accrued during his career would be utilized against the young upstart from Culiacán. "My fight plan," Castillo reported later, "was to outbox Julio. Box, get in and out, and run circles around him."

Castillo's fight plan went out the window in the first round. Chávez cut off the ring immediately and continually, and instead of "running circles around him," Castillo found himself consistently maneuvered onto the ropes and into the corners, where he was forced to trade punches with Chávez. This he did with heroic resolve, but the fighter who can beat Chávez by trading punches with him has yet to emerge. By round 5 Chávez's accuracy and firepower had withered the game Castillo. His mouth was bloodied and he had a cut over his right eye that would require 15 stitches. "Chavez's punches numb you," recalled Castillo. "That's the best way to describe it. They're numbing. And Julio didn't have any idiosyncrasies in the ring. He never gave a signal that a hard punch was coming. He just delivered it." Despite the facial damage, it was Chávez's body blows that hurt Castillo most: "Julio hit me with some hooks to the body, and it felt like I was having epilepsy."

The end came for the battered Castillo in the sixth round. Chávez, sensing that his opponent's strength was waning rapidly, caught him in on the ropes. During the exchange of punches that followed, Chávez unleashed a sudden, violent sequence of blows to the head and body. Three short lefts to the stomach and three short uppercuts to the chin (or, as the writer A. J. Liebling once put it, "three punches between the thorax and abdomen and three to the lower maxillary") dropped the challenger. Castillo struggled to beat the count. He made it to his knees by the count of six. But then, as if the accumulated effects of the punishment he had absorbed suddenly began to flow through his body like a slow-acting poison swallowed an hour before, Castillo's eyes glazed over; an expression of anguish appeared on his face, and he melted, semiconscious, to the floor of the ring, where he remained for several minutes. When he showed signs of regaining his senses, a doctor asked him if he knew where he was. Castillo replied, "I'm in a mess."

"When he's got you hurt, you're done," Castillo said of Chávez. "That's it. He goes for the jugular and he knows how to close escrow. I still have nightmares about Chávez. I hope his dog dies." After Castillo had recovered and returned to his stool, promoter Don King asked if he wanted a rematch. "And I thought," recalls Castillo, "A rematch? Why? Why would I want a rematch?"

"A COUNTRY THEY'VE NEVER BEEN TO"

Benito Juárez, who served as president from 1867 to 1872, was known as the Abraham Lincoln of Mexico. A self-educated scholar and lawyer, Juárez devoted his efforts to modernizing the country and bettering the lot of Mexico's downtrodden peasants, Indians, and mestizos.

A period of order and stability came to Mexico in 1867 when Benito Juárez became president. Juárez was a full-blooded Zapotec Indian from the mountain village of San Paulo Guelatao. Despite the fact that he was an Indian and thus belonged to the group that occupied the lowest rung of Mexico's social ladder, Juárez had managed the unlikely accomplishment of becoming a lawyer and scholar. He spent his early adult years championing the rights of the Mexican peasantry and Indian tribes who had for centuries been exploited by wealthy landowners (including the powerful Catholic church), often offering his services for free. His reputation as a thoughtful and resourceful *hombre de la gente* made him a popular figure among liberal politicians and the majority of mestizos, Indians, and peasants. His leadership and resolve in defeating an invasion by the French in 1862—during which, again, Mexico City was occupied by a foreign army—made him an authentic Mexican hero. Juárez was elected president of Mexico in 1867.

As president, Juárez instituted land-reform laws, nationalized church property, eliminated the pervasive influence of the church in government, rebuilt and established schools across the countryside, constructed

71

a central railway, and discharged two-thirds of the disorganized, corrupt, and dangerous Mexican federal army, which was the equivalent of a loose cannon on the deck of a ship caught in a perpetual storm. The internal violence that had plagued Mexico since 1810 finally died out. But when Benito Juárez himself died suddenly of a heart attack in 1872, anarchy once again engulfed Mexico. The disorder ended with the emergence of General Porfirio Díaz. Díaz had been a troublesome presence in Mexican politics for years, having fallen in and out of favor repeatedly as governments changed hands. He had managed, however, to keep himself alive throughout—a formidable accomplishment in itself. Díaz filled the power vacuum that followed the death of Juárez, and by 1884, he had established himself as El Presidente— Mexico's dictator.

During his 25 years as Mexico's sole ruler, Díaz brought civil order, a healthy, booming economy, modern industrial and agricultural innovations, and foreign investment rather than foreign invasion to his nation. He expanded the rail system immensely, built new ports, and ended the political neutralization of the church that Juárez had instituted. But all this came with a price. The price was any semblance of authentic democracy in Mexico. Porfirio Díaz was, when all was said and done, a dictator, and he ruled with an iron fist.

Roger Mayweather also fancied himself a man with an iron fist. A former junior-lightweight champion, he was often compared—in the early days of his career, at least—to the superb multititle champion Thomas Hearns. Mayweather himself did all he could to facilitate this comparison. Like Hearns, he was considered a talented and dangerous fighter. Unlike Hearns, he was a generally nasty fellow as well. (Mayweather had been banned from fighting in his home state of Michigan for taunting his opponents.) May-

Porfirio Díaz succeeded Juárez as president of Mexico in 1872 and ruled, with only a brief interruption, until 1910. Díaz did much to promote industry in Mexico, but his dictatorial policies benefited the wealthy at the expense of the poor and eventually touched off a revolution.

weather was built much like Hearns—tall and lean, with thin legs and an extremely long reach. Hearns was known as the Motor City Cobra. Mayweather, enamored with the snake motif, had dubbed himself the Black Mamba.

Many boxing pundits were surprised when Julio César Chávez chose to make his second title defense against Mayweather, who was the top-rated challenger in the division. The bout was extremely important for Chávez; not only was Mayweather considered to be his toughest opponent to date, but the fisticuffs would be broadcast on network TV, and thus Chávez was to have his first nationwide exposure in the United States. But many people believed that the Mexican had bitten off more than he could chew; that

Mayweather was exactly the type of fighter Chávez would do best to avoid. He was tall and mobile, featured a stiff, accurate left jab and quick hands, and had one-punch knockout power. Most important, and most ominous for the shorter Chávez, Mayweather had a full four-inch reach advantage over him. This, it was believed, might prove the undoing of the champion from Culiacán.

This opinion was based on the spectacular collision between Thomas Hearns and WBA welterweight champion Pipino Cuevas back in 1980. Cuevas, a tremendously popular knockout artist from Mexico, had run up an impressive string of devastating knockouts, defending his title 13 times. Then he ran into Hearns. Cuevas had a simple style: He came forward against his opponent until he was close enough to engage him in an exchange of punches, during which he would release a right-handed bomb, which, when

Welterweight champion and knockout artist Pipino Cuevas was one of Mexico's great sports heroes during the 1970s. However, on August 2, 1980, both Cuevas's reign as champion and the national pride of Mexico were rudely shattered in the second round by the thunderous right hand of Detroit's Thomas Hearns.

it landed, invariably left his adversary prone on the canvas. He never got close enough to hit Hearns, however, for Hearns had an overwhelming advantage in reach and height. And, despite his lanky build, Hearns himself had a ballistic right hand. During the second round of their encounter, Cuevas was moving in on Hearns in his characteristic manner. The Mexican was only about halfway to his destination when the Cobra dropped a long, straight, whiplash right on Pipino's chin. Cuevas was rendered unconscious so quickly that he did not even have time to fall over. Hearns air-mailed in another overseas right, to aid the force of gravity. Cuevas fell on his face as if whatever it was that animated his body had deserted him and returned to Mexico. It was one of the most devastating knockouts in boxing history, and it effectively ended the career of Cuevas. This scene had permanently etched itself on the minds of boxing fans, writers, trainers, and fighters, much like the right-hand shot from Rocky Marciano that virtually decapitated Jersey Joe Walcott in 1952.

Many members of the press and public were recalling the Hearns-Cuevas scenario as Chávez and Mayweather met in Las Vegas on July 7, 1985. Mayweather, no doubt, was replaying it over and over in his own mind as he prepared for the fight. Chávez, moving inexorably forward as was his style, would walk right into a long-distance right hand delivered by the Mamba. Chávez, however, was not Pipino Cuevas, and Mayweather was no Thomas Hearns.

During the customary prefight instructions at center ring, Mayweather attempted to "stare down" Chávez. He literally stared *down* at the Mexican, who was much shorter than Mayweather. But his attempt at intimidation failed, for his stare was a pathetic version of the truly chilling dead man's gaze that Hearns greeted his opponents with. Mayweather then refused to touch gloves with Chávez. At this, Chávez grinned in a rather malignant fashion. The fighters retired to their corners to await the opening bell.

The first round unfolded just as Chávez's supporters feared it might. Moving in on Mayweather, Chávez was greeted with a long, booming right hand. The punch landed flush on his jaw. Mayweather stepped back and waited for the Mexican to collapse. Chávez irritably looked at Mayweather, moved forward, and whacked the Mamba in the ribs. Mayweather, confused, spent the remainder of the round using his long left to keep Chávez away. When the round ended, Chávez jarred Mayweather with a left-handed chop to the jaw. After the bell sounded, he stood in front of Mayweather and stared at him coldly. He was not smiling now. Chávez remained in front of Mayweather until the Mamba, looking rather perplexed, moved off to his corner.

Round 2 proceeded in an identical manner. Sugar Ray Leonard, who was doing color commentary for the fight, had just remarked on the dangers Chávez faced as he moved inexorably forward, when Mayweather threw his bomb again. Again, it landed flush. This time, however, Chávez leapt inside before the Mamba could recoil and landed a right-hand smash to the jaw that sent Mayweather reeling backward across the ring. Chávez went after him as if Mayweather had insulted the Virgin of Guadalupe. A roundhouse right knocked Mayweather through the ropes. He hung there like an infantryman entangled in a coil of barbed wire. The referee helped the Mamba extricate himself and climb back into the ring. Chávez promptly dropped him with a right to the jaw. Mayweather climbed to his feet; Chávez knocked him back down. Mayweather got up again, tottering in an oddly fluid manner, as if his spine had liquified. In the words of Rubén Castillo, Chávez then "closed escrow." Later, in a classic exam-

Challenger Roger Mayweather (right) was favored to beat Chávez when the two paired off for the WBC super-featherweight title in July 1985. Mayweather was a powerful puncher who enjoyed a four-inch reach advantage over Chávez, but the Mexican walked through Mayweather's punches and knocked him out in the second round.

ple of boxer's understatement, Mayweather summed up the affair: "He refused to respect my punch."

Chávez continued to take on each succeeding number one contender in the division. His next title defenses, fought consecutively with no tune-up bout in between, were two of the toughest in his career. Both were great bouts against a couple of true ring warriors—Rocky Lockridge and Juan LaPorte. For boxing fans, writers, and analysts, these two fights were instrumental in revealing what Julio César Chávez is really all about as a prizefighter.

Boxing analysts have been attempting to define Chávez as a fighter for years. This has proved difficult. Originally, Chávez had been pigeonholed as a pure knockout artist who engaged his opponents in slug-fests and disposed of them via sheer punching power. This erroneous view resulted from Chávez's record of quick knockouts during the first years of his career. These knockouts, in turn, were the result of opponents who knew little of Chávez and who were thus unaware of his punching power. They rushed out to meet him head on, with little regard for defense, and subsequently, as A. J. Liebling would put it, "they quickly went away from their consciousness." Once he was champion, Chávez's opponents began to respect his punching power; they were also of a much better class of fighter—smarter, tougher, more talented in all the various aspects of prizefighting. These opponents brought out the true nature of Chávez as a pugilist. It might be pointed out that, nevertheless, Chávez has stopped more that three-quarters of his opponents in 89 fights to date. But this is due to the fact that Chávez is a great "finisher" rather than a knockout artist. A knockout artist and a finisher are two different animals entirely. A knockout artist is a fighter who depends on the knockout to win. Usually, knockout artists who fail to dispose of their opponent in a given bout wind up losing. A finisher, in boxing terms, is a fighter who invariably "closes escrow" when and if the opportunity arises. But he does not depend on the knockout to win. He is just as content to go the distance and pound out a victory on points. Chávez belongs to the latter group.

Julio César Chávez is a technician, and long bouts allow him to utilize all his skills in his analytical, technical manner. One has not truly seen Julio César Chávez fight until one has seen him in a long bout against a tough opponent. During such a contest, Chávez pursues his opponent in a geometrical pattern, cutting down the ring space with lateral movement. Then, using whatever punches seem most effective for the situation at hand, he delivers them in a manner calculated to gradually but inexorably break down his opponent physically and mentally. He administers the blows with merciless precision, and as his opponent resists, Chávez steadily increases the punishment. He is a cerebral puncher: he knows where and how to hit to inflict pain, to impair breathing, to numb reflexes, to neutralize mobility, to draw blood.

Chávez is also the most psychologically demoralizing of fighters. He seems tireless. It seems impossible to deter him from what he plans to do. A hard punch or combination from an opponent is always answered twofold or threefold by Chávez. And he seems to possess the innate ability to impose himself on a bout. Freddy Brown, Rocky Marciano's cut man, summed up this quality in Marciano: "[Fighting Rocky] is not like playing football. Rocky never gives you the ball." Julio César Chávez never gives you the ball either. What he gives you is the unmistakable impression that the fight is *his*. The ring belongs to *him,* and thus he will dictate what occurs there. The resulting cumulative physiological and psychological effects make the prospect of fighting into the later rounds with Chávez a hellish one, and going the distance with him is a difficult task indeed. The ring is Chávez country; the late rounds are nightfall in Chávez country—a bad time to be abroad in those badlands. As Ferdie Pacheco put it, observing one of Chávez's rapidly withering adversaries answer the bell for the eighth round of a bout, "This is the point where Chávez takes his opponent to a country they've never been to."

Both Rocky Lockridge and Juan LaPorte traveled deep into that country. In his August 3, 1986, bout with Chávez—a bruising war incongruously staged before a diamond-studded audience in the tiny European principality of Monaco with the glamorous Prince Rainier and Princess Caroline in attendance—Lockridge came as close to legitimately beating Chávez as any man ever has. A seasoned veteran and former champion from New Jersey, with a record of 38 and 4 with 32 knockouts, Rocky Lockridge was (and still is, no doubt) as tough as they come. In many ways, Lockridge was similar to Chávez as a fighter. After the bout, he described Chávez as "a great technician but also a thunderous puncher. He can adjust and adapt to any kind of style." This is a pretty good description of Lockridge himself, although Rocky preferred to impose his own style on an opponent rather than adjust. Lockridge was a scaled-down Joe Frazier. He came forward in a relentless manner, using his muscular torso and powerful legs to bull his opponents backward to the ropes or into a corner, where he would proceed to mug them.

The Rock started off strong and stayed toe-to-toe with Chávez throughout. The fight, a trench warfare duel waged by two experts in that grueling style, was even through seven rounds. In the seventh, the two fighters engaged in an extended, center-ring, blow-for-blow exchange that had the polite, dinner-jacketed crowd on its feet and roaring in spite of themselves (the prince remained seated). Neither man would give an inch. The handful of Mexican fans who had come along with the champion's entourage nodded to one another knowingly as the bell rang to end the round. Lockridge was "más macho." Chávez and

Rocky Lockridge connects with a left during his 1986 bout with Chávez in Monaco. A rugged, relentless battler, Lockridge gave Chávez one of his toughest fights, but after 12 grueling rounds the Mexican champion won a close decision from the judges.

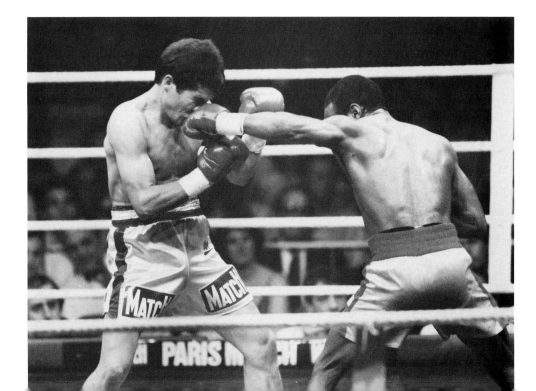

Lockridge looked at one another and slapped gloves in respect before they went to their corners. But in the following round, the ebb and flow of the bout began to change. Chávez got progressively stronger, whereas Lockridge began to slow down. Chávez simply *imposed* himself on the fight, picking up his attack steadily, slipping, blocking, or simply ignoring the punches of Lockridge, hammering Lockridge repeatedly to the body and following with his trademark short uppercuts to the head and mouth. Lockridge launched hard counterattacks, but they became increasingly sporadic and shorter in duration. By the end of the fight, Lockridge was still grinding away at Chávez, but he was bleeding heavily from the mouth, had a nasty cut below one eye, and was taking a thorough beating. After the bout, bruised, cut, and visibly tired but conducting himself as if he had undergone nothing more than a particularly tough day at a construction site, Lockridge praised Chávez as "a courageous champion" and talked about his (Lockridge's) possible next opponent. He was not known as Rocky for nothing. Chávez was awarded a close but unanimous decision. The crowd, having regained its sense of decorum, applauded approvingly but politely. (Rocky Lockridge, a tough character indeed, went on to win the IBF junior-lightweight title in 1988.)

Juan LaPorte was a Puerto Rican American residing in Brooklyn. A former featherweight champion, he had a record of 27 wins and 6 losses, with 14 knockouts. Although his record was not as impressive as Lockridge's, it was more an indication of the quality of the competition he had faced than any lack of prowess on his part. LaPorte was a talented, resourceful fighter. He had fast hands with which he threw hard, accurate combinations, good power in either hand despite his low knockout ratio, excellent ring movement, solid defensive skills, and a tough chin. He

fought a battle royal with Chávez at Madison Square
Garden on December 12, 1986.

LaPorte held a slight edge through the first six
rounds, frequently jolting Chávez with combinations
to the head. Chávez's battle plan was apparent from
the opening bell—pound LaPorte to the body.
LaPorte held his gloves high to protect his head,
leaving his midsection vulnerable, and Chávez me-
thodically, patiently, but relentlessly hammered LaPorte's
liver, ribs, stomach, and chest. Nothing LaPorte did
could deflect Chávez from this course of action, although he continually answered the body punches by
coming over them with hard blows and combinations
to the Mexican's head. By round 6, the body assault
was beginning to have a visible effect on LaPorte. He
was carrying his arms lower and tucking his elbows in
against his ribs to protect them. But he could not
prevent the blows from landing. Chávez always found
an angle to send one, two, or three of them home,
stepping to the left or the right, dipping low by
bending his knees or straightening up as he delivered
his punches. By round 8, LaPorte was suffering. Sometimes a digging hook to the midsection would literally
stop LaPorte cold; he would simply halt his fighting
and stand still. At times, a body shot delivered just as
LaPorte threw a punch to Chávez's head would cause
the punch to simply die on its way to the intended
target, like a rocket running out of fuel mid-flight. By
round 9, his hands had dropped even lower, and
Chávez began mixing in short uppercuts and straight
rights to the mouth and chin. Then it was back to the
body. The number and force of the punches increased
steadily—triple left hooks to LaPorte's ribs followed
immediately by a left uppercut to the chin, with a
straight right to the head, a right to the body, and a left
to the body finishing the combination. LaPorte retali-
ated, but now any punch he landed was responded to

Juan LaPorte, shown here with his son Juan, Jr., after winning the WBC featherweight title in 1982. LaPorte fought a memorable bout with Chávez at New York's Madison Square Garden in 1986. Although LaPorte put up a spirited fight in lasting the distance with Chávez in a losing effort, the effects of going 12 rounds with the Mexican left LaPorte a shell of the fighter he once was.

by Chávez with two, three, or four punches. Still, LaPorte was gritty, and he fought on to the final bell, often landing hard combinations of his own. But when the bell to end the fight sounded, Juan LaPorte was a badly damaged fighter. His face was swollen and his nose was bleeding freely, but the internal torment he felt was the most apparent feature displayed on his face. He was a man in deep inner anguish. There was blood in his urine for weeks after the fight. Chávez, unmarked, was awarded a unanimous decision. Juan LaPorte, for his part, left a piece of himself in that ring. He continued his career, but he was a shell of the fighter he had once been and never regained his status as a serious contender.

By August 1987, Julio César Chávez was 54-0. He had gone through the super-featherweight division like the vengeance of Cuauhtémoc. Little quality opposition was left at the time, and no manager worth his salt was going to send a talented young prospect into the ring with Chávez. (That mistake would be made by Lou Duva three years later.) Don King (who had wooed Chávez away from Felix Ramón after Chávez became champion) arranged for Chávez to challenge Edwin Rosario for Rosario's WBA lightweight title in Las Vegas on November 21, 1987.

Everyone agreed that this would be a difficult challenge for Chávez. He would be moving up to a heavier weight class where the opposition would be physically bigger, stronger, and more powerful. And Rosario was regarded as one of the best pugilists of the day, in the prime of his career. He was also considered to be the hardest-hitting fighter in the lightweight division.

Rosario, a 24-year-old Puerto Rican with a record of 27 victories, 2 losses, and 22 knockouts, made his first mistake well before he stepped into the ring

Puerto Rico's Edwin Rosario (left) made the mistake of verbally taunting Chávez before their lightweight championship match in November 1987. Chávez responded by subjecting Rosario to 11 rounds of brutal punishment that effectively ended Rosario's career as a championship-caliber boxer.

with Chávez. He apparently did not take his opponent seriously, for he insulted Chávez repeatedly before the fight with comments about Chávez's mother, about Mexican women in general, and about Chávez himself. "Chávez will run like a chicken," Rosario said. "I can see it in his face that he is afraid." Chávez's reply was succinct: "I'm going to break your ribs."

Rosario's trash talking resulted in his own personal Día de los Muertos. That night in Las Vegas was perhaps Julio César Chávez's finest hour in the ring. For Rosario, it was a nightmare in which his future as a fighter was literally beaten out of him. The bout was a frightening, analytical massacre from the opening bell, during which Chávez unleashed his entire arsenal. Chávez was cold, calculating, and merciless. He did not rush into the ring and immediately attempt to knock out Rosario. He steadily *reduced* him, punch by punch, combination by combination, round by round. Home Box Office (HBO) commentator Sugar Ray Leonard remarked that Chávez's body attack was like watching "a man chop down a tree," and by the ninth round, fellow commentator Barry Tompkins characterized the bout as an "abattoir" (slaughterhouse). About all that can be said for Rosario's performance is that he lasted into the 11th round and remained on his feet throughout. By the ninth round, however, he was bleeding profusely from the mouth and nose; his face had changed shape as if, in the words of sportswriter Phil Berger, "he'd been set upon by a horde of bees"; and the one eye that was not swollen shut was alarmingly vacant. In the 10th, members of the audience began to implore the referee to stop the fight. Early in the 11th, a vicious right hand by Chávez sent Rosario's bloody mouthpiece spinning off into the crowd. Rosario's trainer then threw a towel into the ring, ending the slaughter. "He did the right thing," Sugar Ray somberly commented.

THE HARD RAIN

Despite the political stability and industrial growth brought about by the three decades of the Porfiriato, as the dictatorship of Díaz was known, the plight of the mestizos and Indians of Mexico only worsened. The economic benefits of industrialization and the influx of foreign capital only made the rich of Mexico richer, while the ever-increasing millions of peasants—Mexico's population had reached 13 million by 1910, the overwhelming majority of whom were mestizo—remained virtually landless, disenfranchised, and brutally exploited as agricultural and industrial laborers.

In 1910, the situation exploded. Revolution, followed by nightmarish civil war, once again wracked Mexico. The next 10 years were perhaps the worst in Mexico's long history of inner turmoil. Over a million Mexicans died in this crucible, including the best of that nation's legendary defenders of the downtrodden. Francisco Madero, the man whose heartfelt empathy for Mexico's exploited masses finally sparked the initial revolution that led to the downfall and exile of Díaz, was elected president only to be betrayed and assassinated by his own generals. This set off a bitter sequence of infighting between the revolutionary forces; a vicious struggle that resembled, in its bloody cycle of betrayals and murders, a cross between a Shakespear-

Chávez celebrates his TKO over Roger Mayweather in May 1989. After 11 brutal rounds with Chávez, Mayweather simply quit on his stool. Though Chávez was by now acknowledged by many experts as one of the best fighters in the world, he was just beginning to enjoy the widespread admiration of his fellow Mexicans.

ean political tragedy and a Mafia power struggle. The notorious bandit-revolutionary, Pancho Villa, was defeated by the forces of Álvaro Obregón after two blood-drenched battles in 1915. Villa was eventually assassinated. Emiliano Zapata, the greatest of Mexico's revolutionary fighters, along with his loyal army, was finally defeated by the combined forces of Obregón and Venustiano Carranza. Zapata fled to the hills with the remnants of his army to wage guerrilla warfare. In April 1919, Zapata was betrayed; he rode into an ambush and was riddled with bullets. As the news of his murder spread across the countryside that night, peasants wept openly. Obregón then turned on Carranza and had him murdered. In 1920, Álvaro Obregón became Mexico's first dominant *caudillo,* or political boss, since Díaz. He ruthlessly crushed a final uprising in 1923, executing all those who were involved. Obregón imposed a measure of stability until 1928, when he was assassinated by an irate cartoonist. Obregón's vice-president, Plutarco Elías Calles (whom many believed was behind the cartoonist's actions) then came to power. He was eventually deposed and sent into exile by one of the last of the true hombres de la gente, a mestizo, General Lázaro Cárdenas, who was elected president in 1934. It was Cárdenas who finally led the deeply embittered and cynical peoples of Mexico on their first steps toward a relatively secure and cohesive nationhood.

By 1990, Julio César Chávez had done what he had promised himself as a teenager that he would do. He had shouldered the burden of providing security for a large family in a violent and impoverished environment. And he had done so in a manner and to a degree that would have been beyond the wildest dreams of anyone in dusty, thirsty, bullet-riddled Culiacán. At age 28, he had firmly established himself as the best prizefighter on the planet. Following his

Soldiers in the revolutionary army of Pancho Villa, photographed in 1914. After the fall of Porfirio Díaz in 1910, Mexico endured 10 years of civil war; at the end of that bitter struggle, the nation took its first steps toward stability under President Álvaro Obregón.

destruction of Edwin Rosario, he had gone on to win the WBC lightweight championship by defeating fellow countryman José Luis Ramírez in a hard battle in Las Vegas in October 1988, thus unifying the WBC and WBA lightweight titles. Six months later, he had stepped up in weight class again to capture the WBC super-lightweight title from his old friend Roger Mayweather. The former Black Mamba had apparently learned nothing from his previous encounter with Chávez. For his title defense against Chávez, he had, remarkably, adopted the nickname the Mexican Assassin. Chávez did not appear offended by this; rather, he seemed quite amused. Nevertheless, he proceeded to beat mercilessly on Mayweather's midsection as if he were a stubborn mule and to open a cut over Mayweather's eye that gaped like the mouth of a fish out of water. By round 8, Mayweather was having trouble breathing, and in between rounds 9 and 10 he could not keep his mouthpiece in his mouth because he was experiencing violent stomach spasms due to the bodily pounding he had received. Mayweather spit the bit after round 10. Doubled over in pain on his stool, he declined to answer the bell for the next round. There was a "Mexican Assassin" in the ring that night, but it was not Roger Mayweather.

Thus, by early 1990, Chávez had a record of 68-0 and held four world titles. In 10 years as a professional, he was unbeaten. Ring historians searched in vain to find a similar record. Chávez was now earning half-million-dollar purses for championship defenses and

Chávez rocks José Luis Ramírez with a short left hook during their October 1988 bout in Las Vegas, Nevada. With his victory over Ramírez, Chávez unified the WBC and WBA lightweight titles and took another step toward boxing immortality.

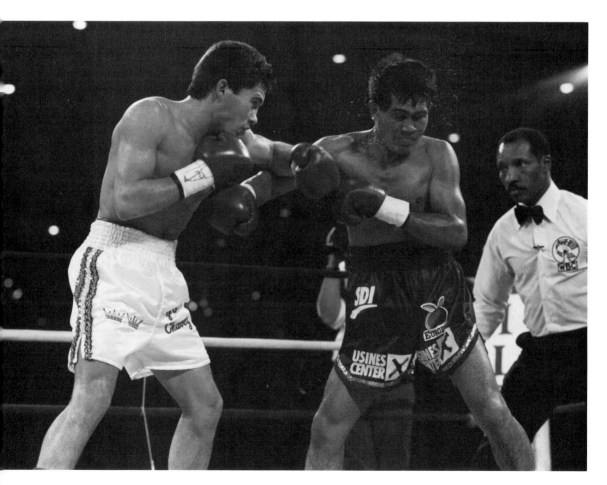

challenges, and averaging about $100,000 per nontitle bout. Because he had steadily maintained his rigorous fighting schedule—he had averaged a fight every 57 days for 10 years—he was now a rich man.

From the beginning, Chávez had used his earnings to provide for his family, which was growing steadily. (Chávez and his wife, Amalia, the Culiacán beauty who was his childhood sweetheart, were married in 1985; they now have three sons, Christian, Omar, and Julio, Jr.) "First," Chávez recalled in an interview in *Penthouse* magazine, "I bought the land that the railroad car was on. Then I built a new house for my parents. Every bit of money I made in boxing went to that house." As the victories and title belts piled up, so did the money. Chávez built a house for his wife and children. He bought a restaurant for his mother and sister, a gas station for two of his brothers, a pool hall for another, an auto repair shop for yet another, and a discotheque for another sister. He employed other brothers, uncles, and amigos as trainers, training camp attendants, or supervisors of the real estate he was investing in and building on in Culiacán. He bought apartments, houses, and cars for them all. Every year on April 30, Mexico's Day of the Children, he gave away boxes of toys to the poor children of Culiacán. "Ever since he was a very little boy," his mother says, "he has had this idea that he must take care of all the people around him. He was the little father of our family." "He is our saint," his sister Perla adds. "He solves all our problems."

There was one thing that Chávez had not accomplished, however. Curiously, he had not yet received the recognition he was due from his fellow Mexicans. This odd and seemingly inexplicable phenomenon was frequently commented on by the North American boxing press. How was it that a boxer in a boxing-crazy nation in a boxing-crazy part of the world—a

Chávez and his wife, Amalia, admire their newborn son, Christian, outside the family home in Culiacán. Chávez not only provides for his wife and three children but for all his relatives and numerous friends and associates. "He is our saint," his sister Perla has remarked. "He solves all our problems."

fighter who was generally recognized outside his country as the best pound-for-pound fighter in the world and who was on the verge of establishing himself as one of the greatest fighters in the history of the sport: how was it that this man was not a national hero in his own nation, as Roberto Durán had been in Panama and Alexis Arguëllo had been in Nicaragua? Chávez had long since eclipsed the accomplishments of those two Latino champions. Chávez did have a faithful following in Mexico, but he had yet to receive anything compared to the national respect and honors Durán and Arguëllo had received. Indeed, Pipino Cuevas, who was retired, and Salvador Sánchez, who was long dead, were still more popular than Chávez. How could this be?

Various reasons were postulated. Some journalists believed it was because Chávez had been underpromoted by Don King. For most of Chávez's career with King as his manager and promoter, King had been preoccupied with the promotion of heavyweight Mike Tyson. Thus, Chávez had fought few headline bouts, usually finding himself on heavyweight undercards. Others attributed Chávez's lack of recognition to his personality. They said that he simply had no charisma, both inside and outside the ring. Unlike Cuevas, whose booming knockouts appealed to Mexicans, and Sánchez, who fought with a kind of natural dash and daring, Chávez was unspectacular in the ring. He fought like a man with a job to do, like a technician. The subtleties of his style, and his warrior's heart, were overshadowed by the methodical precision with which he went about his work. Despite his overwhelming accomplishments, he seemed like just another one of the hundreds of hardworking, blue-collar Mexican fighters. Outside the ring, there was nothing for the press to latch onto that would bring Chávez any additional attention. After a fight, he went home to Culiacán. He was a devoted family man with a successful marriage. His daily life revolved around business, his wife, his children, and training for the inevitable next bout. His nightlife consisted of drinking a few cold beers and listening to mariachi music in the street in front of his house with his *compañeros.* There were no scandals, no drugs, no illicit affairs with movie stars, no brawls in nightclubs, no car accidents, no controversial political statements. In interviews, Chávez was soft-spoken, friendly, and polite. Although he had grown up in an environment that was similar to Mike Tyson's, he was no Mike Tyson. Indeed, he was the direct opposite of Tyson.

All of these explanations have merit and no doubt contributed to the lack of recognition Chávez experienced in the United States, but they do not explain the situation in his home country. (The most salient reason for Chávez's lack of recognition in the United States was simply that he was from another country. How many foreign athletes are recognized in the United States?) Mexico's initial reluctance to embrace Chávez has more to do with deeply rooted elements of Mexican culture and national identity. In *Distant Neighbors,* Alan Riding has discussed the all-pervasive influence of Mexico's troubled past on its present and on its view of the future: "The disasters that befall Mexico are considered unavoidable. . . . The country's own historical record of defeats and betrayals has prepared Mexicans to expect and accept the worst. [Mexican] heroes, from Cuauhtémoc to Zapata, have been murdered." Mexican poet Octavio Paz wrote of Mexico that "the hero's tomb is the cradle of the people. We are nihilists [people without faith], except that our nihilism is not intellectual but instinctive, and therefore irrefutable."

And therein lies the reason for the wariness with which the Mexican people regarded Julio César Chávez. It would be simplistic—and insulting to Mexicans—to think that Mexicans withheld their adulation of Chávez for so long for reasons as ultimately trivial as boxing style and a lack of tabloid charisma. This would be the equivalent of Americans withholding their adulation of Joe DiMaggio if, for instance, he had never married Marilyn Monroe. Mexico is a nation of boxing aficionados; knowledgeable boxing fans, much like the average American is rather alarmingly knowledgeable about baseball. Mexicans were all too aware that in Chávez, they had a diamond in their midst, something special and unprecedented. But their deeply ingrained sense of cultural fatalism, the scars of their dark history, the "instinctive nihilism" spoken of by Paz, made them afraid to release the true feelings they were beginning to feel, on a nationwide level, for this remarkable man

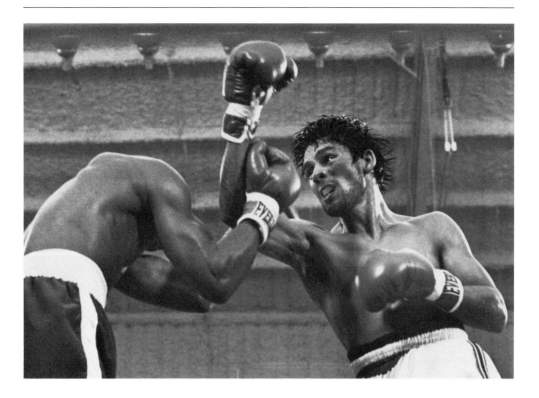

Known as Manos de Piedra (Hands of Stone), the great Roberto Durán (right) became a national hero in his native Panama when he won the lightweight title in 1972. Asked in a recent interview about his own "dream fight," Chávez responded immediately: "Me versus Roberto Durán! I tell you, we would take it to each other."

from Culiacán. As Alan Riding observed, in Mexico, "when ancient and modern [in this case, age-old despair and a new hero] clash, emotions invariably favor the past." More simply put, Chávez was too good to be true. Could something *this good* actually be happening to Mexico, they asked themselves. Chávez, in the story of his life and his performance in the ring, in his refusal to accept things that other Mexicans instinctively accepted and expected, in his *undefeatedness,* negated a fatalism so old and deeply ingrained that the resulting tension between the two forces caused a kind of culture shock for Mexicans. Thus, Mexicans were *afraid* to embrace Chávez, for if they did he would surely be killed in a car accident, like Sánchez; or he would be knocked cold by some new Thomas Hearns, like Cuevas. He would meet disaster, like all Mexican heroes.

These were powerful cultural undercurrents for a single man, a mere boxer, to overcome. Yet overcome them Chávez did. Much as he fought, patiently, tirelessly, willfully, punch by punch, round by round, fight by fight, he wore away at the feelings of his reluctant countrymen and -women. Things started to change with the Rosario fight. Mexican fight fans and fighters harbor a deep contempt for Puerto Rican boxers; they consider them trash talkers and nonfighters. When Rosario insulted Mexican women and was subsequently pulverized by Chávez, Mexicans quietly took notice. When an American calling himself the Mexican Assassin hit Chávez flush on the jaw with an uppercut thrown from his heels, only to have Chávez nod to him approvingly, as if to say "not bad," and then beat him into submission by the 10th round, Mexicans were watching more closely. On March 17, 1990, when Chávez fought IBF super-lightweight champion Meldrick Taylor, who had somehow managed to become acclaimed as Chávez's equal as a fighter, Mexicans were watching *very* closely.

There was much talk in America about the Chávez-Taylor fight, both before and immediately after the bout. Nobody talks about it much anymore, however—at least not north of the border. Meldrick Taylor, at the age of 23, was one of the prize jewels of promoter-manager Lou Duva's stable of talented boxers. An Olympic hero with a professional record of 23 victories, no losses, and a draw, Taylor had been built up by the boxing press and Duva as one of the best fighters in the world. The Chávez-Taylor bout was ballyhooed by the sports press in the United States as the first great fight of the 1990s, a contest between two men who were perhaps the best in their field. In reality, the fight was a long sequence of misjudgments, misrepresentations, and manipulations, as Don King might say.

The victim was Meldrick Taylor. A gifted fighter, Taylor might one day have become one of the best in the world. His *potential* was unlimited. His true capabilities as a prizefighter, unfortunately, were not. The most serious misjudgment was on the part of manager Lou Duva. Duva never should have sent Taylor into the ring against Chávez. The young man simply was not yet equipped for that type of storm. Duva, like a large portion of the American sports press, harbored a deep resentment of Chávez. On Duva's part, the resentment stemmed from the Rocky Lockridge fight. Duva, who managed Lockridge, was convinced that his fighter had won his fight against Chávez and that he and Lockridge had been "robbed" by the judges. Since then, Duva had developed an obsession with Chávez that resembled Captain Ahab's mania for killing the white whale in Herman Melville's *Moby Dick*. This must have clouded his vision about the dangers of sending Taylor, at his present stage of development as a professional boxer, into the ring with Chávez. The U.S. sports media was glad to jump on board Duva's *Pequod,* for they were already well into their Great American Hope phase, which would eventually manifest itself in some extremely disturbing journalism. The boxing press in particular hyped Taylor and downplayed Chávez, thus reinforcing Duva's delusions. Taylor was thus sent to "a country he'd never been to" without a map. Nightfall came, and he got lost. He never came back.

March 17 was a great night for Julio César Chávez, an embarrassing night for three HBO sportscasters and three judges, a bad night for Lou Duva, and a tragic one for Meldrick Taylor. In 12 rounds of boxing, Chávez not only exposed Taylor's deficiencies as a pugilist; he gave him the worst beating he has ever administered to a fighter in a long career that has featured many a destructive evening. The announcers,

Sugar Ray Leonard, Jim Lampley, and Larry Merchant, exposed themselves as presenting a disgracefully one-sided view of the fight that had absolutely nothing to do with what was actually occurring in the ring. As the contest progressed, they repeatedly declared that Taylor was "dominating the fight," "controlling the tempo," "outpunching Chávez," and so on, ad nauseum. Replays of the fight reveal that they failed to notice, or chose not to comment on, Chávez's defense, which often made Taylor look amateurish. In one round, Taylor threw over 700 punches and landed less than 300; in another, Chávez casually stepped back

Chávez's association with promoter Don King (left), which began in 1984, may have been responsible for his struggle to achieve recognition. King did not begin to promote Chávez as a headline fighter until his principal meal ticket, heavyweight Mike Tyson, went to prison on a rape charge.

from one of Taylor's schoolyard left hooks, causing Taylor to fall to the floor. (One of the more comical interludes occurred just as Larry Merchant was commenting on Taylor, who, "like all Philadelphia fighters, had a great left hook." At that moment, a slow-motion replay was showing Taylor throwing a left hook that missed Chávez by a good 12 inches.) Nor did the announcers notice that the majority of Taylor's punches, when they did land, were poorly thrown, slapping blows that Chávez hardly noticed; or that Taylor was repeatedly and quite obviously shaken and pained by Chávez's blows in virtually every round; and, most important and inexplicable, they hardly said a word about the fact that Chávez had turned the fight into a bloodbath by the seventh round.

The disintegration of Taylor's face was truly horrific. Using primarily a stiff, hacking left jab and a short left uppercut, along with the trademark left hooks to the body, Chavez literally destroyed Taylor. Taylor himself showed remarkable courage and resiliency, but his vaunted hand speed was nullified by a lack of power, gross inaccuracy, and Chávez's defense—and his footwork was nonexistent. He had no defense to speak of. The three announcers ignored all of this—as they did the frightening quantities of blood that was flying around the ring every time Chávez hit Taylor, so much so that Chávez's cornermen had to wash Taylor's blood off *Chávez* in between rounds—as well as the frantic work that went on in Taylor's corner in between rounds to control the facial and cranial swelling, bleeding from the nose and mouth, and multiple lacerations that Taylor suffered.

When the 10th round arrived, Ferdie Pacheco looked over into Taylor's corner: "What I saw shocked me," Pacheco recalled. "His features were horribly disfigured from the cumulative effect of all the blows that Chávez had been landing. It looked like a hard

rain had been wearing away at his face for years." The
HBO announcers, in the meantime, were informing
viewers that according to their scoring, Taylor had
won *all 10 rounds of the fight*. The official judges, as
well, had Taylor inexplicably ahead, although the mar-
gin was much slimmer—he had a slight edge on two
of three cards. Lou Duva let his fighter go out for the
11th, a round that left Taylor so dazed that he had to
be led back to his corner by the referee when the bell
rang. The fight should have been stopped at this point,
by a ring physician, Duva, or the referee. Instead, the
ghastly figure of Meldrick Taylor was allowed to answer the bell for the 12th. Chávez, who had been
informed that this fighter he had just wrecked was
actually *ahead* on the judges' scorecards, was no doubt
enraged, and he went in for the kill, pounding Taylor
around the ring and, with three seconds to go on the
time clock, flooring him violently in a corner with a
perfect right hand, which shattered the orbital bone
around Taylor's left eye. Remarkably, Taylor pulled
himself to his feet by using the ropes. The referee
asked Taylor if he wanted to continue. Taylor, peering
dazedly about and looking much like a figure who
had just stumbled away from an accident, did not
answer. The referee finally, mercifully, stopped the
fight. Chávez, who was unscathed, had won his fifth
world championship. Meldrick Taylor was taken to the
closest hospital, where emergency-room personnel
did indeed assume, before they found out who he was,
that the unfortunate young man had been in a particularly nasty automobile accident.

There was much petulant braying in the U.S.
sporting press that Taylor had been cheated; that there
were only three seconds on the time clock when the
fight was stopped; that Taylor had beaten the count,
and had the referee allowed the bout to conclude,
Taylor would have won because he was ahead on

points when the round started. But the talk soon died down and faded out. Even if Taylor had been ahead on two out of three cards, the beating he took in the final round, coupled with the knockdown and the condition Taylor was in when he arose, would have put Chávez further ahead on the third card and most likely ahead on one and probably two of the others. Some sportswriters may well have obtained a videotape of the bout and replayed it without the inane commentary of the announcers, and thus got a clear view of what kind of carnage was actually occurring in the ring that night. News of Meldrick Taylor's condition began to filter back as well: shattered cheekbone; eyes swollen shut; multiple lacerations of the tongue, lips, inner mouth, and face; two pints of blood left behind in the ring. Taylor's comeback attempt the following year silenced most of the remaining critics. He was knocked out in the early rounds of his first two fights—once by a journeyman boxer few people had ever heard of (Crisanto España). Meldrick Taylor is young; perhaps he can still make it back, although currently he is inactive. Lou Duva still insists that he was "robbed." Meldrick Taylor was indeed robbed that night, but not by Julio César Chávez or the referee.

"BRING US
THE HEAD OF
MACHO CAMACHO"

As a supporter waves the Mexican flag, Chávez celebrates his 1991 victory over Lonnie Smith. He was labeled as a pure brawler earier in his career, but Chávez is a true ring scientist— "Julio understands precisely where to hit people," explains his orthopedist, Dr. Sergio Sandoval. "I swear he knows as much about the vital organs and the nervous system as I do."

President Lázaro Cárdenas provided the ever-growing Mexican masses with authentic hope for the future of the country. A leader with a true empathy for Mexico's downtrodden Indians and mestizos and a visionary with a true belief that Mexico could become a great nation, he changed the face of Mexico forever. He appropriated 46 million acres of land and set it aside for use by previously landless Mexicans. He supported established labor unions and sponsored new ones, such as the civil servant's union, known as the National Confederation of Popular Organizations. Cárdenas also formed the National Peasant Confederation to provide the peasantry with their own political power base. He nationalized the railroad industry, which had become dominated by foreign interests, and in 1938, in the act he is most remembered and honored for, he nationalized Mexico's booming oil industry. Before he left office in 1939, he succeeded in bringing Mexico's four most important and previously contentious political forces—labor, the military, the popular (or middle) class, and the peasantry—into a single national political party, the Institutional Revolutionary Party, which still dominates Mexico today. The years of anarchy were over.

Cárdenas was followed by Manuel Ávila Camacho and then Miguel Alemán Valdés. These leaders, while steering Mexico away from the leftist reforms of Cárdenas, were careful not to undo their predecessor's accomplishments, and by the end of World War II, Mexico was indeed on its way toward joining the modern world. Presidents Adolfo Ruiz Cortines, Adolfo López Mateos, and Gustavo Díaz Ordaz oversaw a new boom in Mexico's economy, the growth of a substantial middle class, new breakthroughs in foreign relations, the construction of better schools, highways, and buildings, a continued, if limited, policy of land reform for the peasantry, and the birth of Mexico's lucrative tourist industry. By the 1960s, Mexico was in many ways a new nation.

Julio César Chávez's victory over Meldrick Taylor pushed him ever closer to superstardom in Mexico. Now Mexicans watched his every fight with growing wonder and enthusiasm. They began to refer to him as "J. C. Superstar." The momentum continued to build throughout 1990, 1991, and 1992, as Chávez rolled his record up to a phenomenal 82-0, scoring knockouts or technical knockouts over 10 of his next 11 opponents. But Mexico wanted one more thing from Chávez before they truly opened themselves up to him. One gift. Bring us the head of Macho Camacho, they demanded.

During a 1935 demonstration in Mexico City, supporters of President Lázaro Cárdenas burn a coffin representing foreign business interests. Cárdenas became a Mexican hero when he nationalized Mexico's oil industry.

Hector "Macho" Camacho had long been the archvillain of Mexican fight fans. He embodied every sterotypical image of Puerto Rican fighters that Mexican fight fans harbored. He was the trash talker of all trash talkers. He was flamboyant in a manner that no fighter since Ali had dared to be, both in and out of the ring. In public he dressed like a neon sign on the front of a Miami discotheque. He wore into the ring outfits that defy description, gyrating his hips to a pounding Latin beat. His bizarre hairstyles changed with each fight. And he talked. He talked before, during, and after his bouts.

Worst of all, this Mexican boxing fan's nightmare could fight. He appeared, seemingly out of nowhere, in 1985, to effortlessly relieve the very popular Mexican José Luis Ramírez of his WBC lightweight title in Las Vegas. He did so with a display of breathtaking hand speed; hand speed that did not, as that type of speed often does, sacrifice accuracy and power. When the young Camacho unleashed a blinding flurry of punches, they landed, which is a rarity. And they landed hard. Camacho also sported the best legs since Ali; he glided about the ring effortlessly and creatively, with sudden, utterly unpredictable changes of direction. He might be sliding out of punching range and then, with seemingly impossible quickness, he would be on his opponent, using his adversary's head as a boxing-gym speed bag. Then he was gone again. And when he chose to, he would stop moving, set his legs, and *hit*. Indeed, in his first years, as a lightweight, Camacho was one of the most naturally gifted boxers to appear in a long time.

But the Macho Man squandered his gift. Too many late nights, too little training, too few fights. He seemed to take nothing seriously, resulting in several brushes with the law and a palpable erosion of his ring skills. Nevertheless, he retained his flamboyance and his overinflated self-opinion. And he retained enough of his natural talent to achieve a record of 39 victories and 1 loss by the time Chávez caught up with him on September 12, 1992.

Despite the fact that the Hector Camacho of 1992 was clearly in over his head with Chávez, something about the matchup appealed to the public, resulting in the fastest ticket sellout for a fight in Las Vegas history. There were few surprises in this fight; Chávez delivered to Mexico not only the head, but the liver, stomach, and ribs of Macho Camacho. The only true surprise was the heart of Camacho—and the graciousness he displayed following the worst beating of his career. In round 10, with Camacho's face swollen, one eye closed, a nasty gash in the other eyelid, and, no doubt, a feeling of deep pain in his body, his cornermen urged him to retire. Camacho refused, and instead went out and battled with Chávez for the final two rounds, actually having his best round of the fight in the 11th.

Following the bout, Camacho had only praise for Chávez. He was obviously in awe of the champion. "He won it, no doubt," Camacho said. "The pressure he put on me was amazing. He's a great fighter."

Strangely, the fight with Chávez seems to have been the best thing that could have happened to Camacho, despite the beating he received. He joined the champion that evening for the victory party and later visited Culiacán for a few days as Chávez's guest. Camacho had learned something from Chávez during the fight, and he seemed eager to know more. Perhaps a lesson in dedication and hard work, in how to be a champion, was being learned. Camacho, who had been written off by the boxing press and who had alienated boxing fans with his behavior over the years, saw his stock as a fighter rise following the fight. His courage had not gone unnoticed. Boxing journalists were writing good things about him. The Macho Man put in a stellar performance in his next bout, and will no doubt soon get another crack at a title.

Julio César Chávez, for his part, returned to Mexico as a national hero of unprecedented proportions. His fellow Mexicans had finally given in, and when they did, the floodgates opened. A national holiday was declared by Mexican president Carlos Salinas de Gortari, and millions of Mexicans filled the streets and the Zócalo to await the arrival of Chávez, who would

Hector "Macho" Camacho displays one of his flamboyant ring outfits before a 1990 bout in Madison Square Garden. Mexican fight fans detested the brash Macho Man; when Chávez thrashed him soundly in 1992, millions of people filled the streets of Mexico City to welcome the victor home.

be received by the president himself at the National Palace. As a helicopter descended with Julio César Chávez aboard, the chant went up from Mexico City, millions of voices chanting in unison, "CHA-vez! CHA-vez! CHA-vez!" The chanting still echoed in February 1993, when Chávez met Greg Haugen in Aztec Stadium.

It was evident immediately that Chávez had come to this fight with what Mike Tyson aptly described as "bad intentions." Though his face is usually a mask of concentration before a bout, his Indian-black eyes virtually sparkled with anticipation. He bounced up and down and pounded his gloves together violently and impatiently. As the two fighters were called to the center of the ring by the referee for the traditional last-minute instructions, Haugen and Chávez came face to face. Haugen attempted to stare down the champion, assuming a tough-guy expression apparently acquired from viewing too many James Cagney gangster movies.

When the referee at Aztec had finished his instructions, Chávez refused with a disdainful gesture the traditional touching of gloves with his opponent and returned to his corner. He pounded his gloves together, his eyes now locked on Haugen. Haugen's "look" had vanished; he now wore the expression of a little boy whistling his way past a particularly spooky graveyard on a particularly dark night. The bell rang.

The fighters met at center ring. Haugen threw a series of tentative left jabs and a short right. Chávez responded with a straight right hand to Haugen's mouth that knocked Haugen a good five feet backward. The punch did not cause Haugen to backpedal or stumble backward; the position of his legs never changed. Rather, he seemed to have been blown backward, as if by a strong gust of wind. Chávez then slammed a left hook to Haugen's ribs and planted a thudding right on his temple that knocked Haugen violently to the canvas. Twenty seconds had passed since the opening bell.

The crowd reacted with pandemonium. Haugen was up quickly, but the expression on his face resembled the confused, startled, and somewhat comical look of a person who has been abruptly awakened from a deep sleep by a sudden, loud noise. Chávez could have finished Haugen off at this point, for Haugen's thought processes were clearly scrambled, and his legs were stiff and locked, refusing to respond to the signals that his instincts for self-preservation were transmitting to them. But instead of moving in for the knockout, Chávez took a step backward and waited for Haugen to regain his senses. Greg Haugen had done a lot of talking before the bout. Now he had to answer for it.

And answer for it he did. Terrific lefts to Haugen's ribs and liver were followed by arrow-straight left-right combinations to his face. The punches to the body of the American were particularly brutal; their effect on him was evident on his face each time one—or two or three of them in combination—landed. Haugen appeared on the verge of going down again several times, but at these moments, Chávez would step back, clearly intending to make the fight last in order to teach his disrespectful opponent a lesson.

Rounds 2, 3, and 4 saw Chávez showcasing his entire arsenal: left hooks to the midsection; short left uppercuts to the solar plexus and the chin; a stiff, cruel left jab to the eyes and mouth; left and right hooks to the elbows, biceps, deltoids, heart, and shoulders; the straight right to the face; and always the digging left hooks to the body. The punches came from every angle and in a variety of combinations. When Haugen came out of the defensive shell he had crawled into— gloves covering his face, elbows tucked in against his body to protect his ribs—and threw punches, Chávez would drive him to the ropes and unleash withering combinations. The crowd, in the meantime, chanted "MAY-hee-co! MAY-hee-co! MAY-hee-co!"

Haugen returned to his corner after the fourth round looking as if he had fought 12 rounds with the merciless champion. He bled from his mouth, his nose, and his left ear. His face was cut in a number of places and seemed to be changing shape. His arms had been pounded into uselessness; he could barely push them forward to punch with. What his innards felt like, only he knew. Haugen was literally and figuratively in a country he'd never been to. For a moment, as he sat in his corner, oblivious to the instructions of his trainer and his assistants, an expression of profound physical anguish, followed by one of resignation, passed over Haugen's features, and it seemed the fight was over. But when the bell rang for the fifth, Greg Haugen answered it.

Julio César Chávez, in the meantime, had apparently decided to end Haugen's torment. An underhand right to the chin made the American's legs dance crazily, like a marionette on a string. A classic combination followed: a short right uppercut to the solar plexus followed by a left hook and a chopping right to the chin. Haugen went down hard. The crowd erupted like one of Mexico's many volcanos. Chávez turned to his fans and pumped a gloved fist in the air. Meanwhile, to his everlasting credit, Greg Haugen managed to haul himself to his feet before the referee reached the count of 10. The referee, for some unfathomable reason, did not stop the fight, nor did Haugen's trainer throw a towel into the ring. The referee waved the two fighters forward.

Now Chávez showed the quality of mercy. Haugen was dazed, battered, and utterly defenseless. Chávez could have unleashed the kind of murderous combi-

Chávez exults after knocking out Greg Haugen at Aztec Stadium in February 1993. "All of Mexico trusts me now," he had told a reporter before the fight. "All of Mexico is depending on me. . . . I cannot fail them."

nation that probably would have resulted in Haugen's removal from the ring on a stretcher. Instead, he backed Haugen up against the ropes and hit him with a rapid series of punches designed to leave stinging welts on his face as a final message to take home to the United States, but Chávez did not attempt to hammer Haugen to the canvas again. Finally, the referee stepped in and stopped the fight. As the crowd stood and roared and the ring filled with adoring fans who lifted Chávez to their shoulders, word went out across Mexico: Chávez remained unvanquished. The new fire burned bright. In Tijuana, the din of taxi drivers blowing their horns could be heard all night long.

A MAN OF MEXICO

On September 11, 1993, in Mexico City's Zócalo, five days before the annual celebration of Mexico's Independence Day, the inhabitants of one of the world's largest tent cities began settling in for the night. According to Tim Golden, a correspondent for the *New York Times,* the tent city is filled with "landless peasants and bankrupt cattle ranchers, laborers laid off by the state . . . thousands of poor farmers, university students and laid off oil workers. . . . 'Where we live, they have us like this,' a 67-year-old peasant named Fortunado Soberana said, grinding his sandal slowly on the paving stones."

Things have changed for the better in Mexico since the days of terror, anarchy, and revolution. But many things remain the same. For millions, Mexico remains a hard place, where survival on a day-to-day basis is a way of life. But the remarkable resiliency of the Mexican people remains the same as well. Their fatalism masks an inner toughness that has enabled them to grow as a nation, despite all odds. In 1968, a similar demonstration in the Zócalo was dispersed by the gunfire of government troops. In today's Mexico, that would be unthinkable. And despite the discontent of the tent city inhabitants, all of them, if questioned, would profess a fierce loyalty to their nation. Among themselves, they may express their discontent and

Trainer Cristobál Rosas laces up Chávez's gloves as the Mexican superstar prepares for a free public workout at Manhattan's Riverbank State Park in August 1993. The event, attended by enthusiastic local residents, testified to Chávez's growing worldwide celebrity.

113

unhappiness with their government's economic policies. But if a foreigner came among them and insulted
their homeland, he would suffer a fate similar to that
of Greg Haugen. From the crucible of their history,
Mexicans have emerged with a deep love and loyalty
for their country. This, ultimately, will make Mexico a
great nation.

As the reporter made his rounds of the tent city on
September 11, Julio César Chávez faced the latest
Great American Hope, Pernell "Sweet Pea" Whitaker,
another of Lou Duva's fighters. The bout was held at
the Alamodome in San Antonio, Texas. The North
American press had portrayed Whitaker as the most
sublime ring artist since Sugar Ray Robinson. But
Chávez, before the fight, called him an "ugly fighter."
Chávez's interpretation was correct.

Pernell Whitaker is a will-o'-the-wisp, a fighter
who has perfected the art of not fighting and, more
important, of not getting hit. His elusiveness and
creativity in avoiding punches is remarkable. Whitaker
does not fight; he wages surprise attacks from unex-
pected angles, uses his fast hands to pepper his opponent, and then vanishes before the other fighter can
retaliate. He does this very well; well enough to have
unified the lightweight title, won the IBF junior-
welterweight title, and won the WBC welterweight
title. Whitaker can make a slow-moving fighter
look positively foolish; and once he has exhausted
opponents by inducing them to chase him around all
night, he turns mean. Because he lacks the punching
power to knock out a beaten opponent, he instead
humiliates him. Whitaker is under the impression
that this aspect of his fighting persona is entertaining; it is, in fact, simply ugly. Despite his achievements in the ring, he has difficulty drawing decent
crowds; his penchant for humiliating his opponents
is one reason for this.

Chávez signs autographs for young fans after sparring several rounds at Riverbank State Park. Having assured the security of his own family, Chávez now donates a substantial portion of his boxing income to organizations that aid Mexican disaster victims, needy children, and the elderly.

The other reason Whitaker has never been a big draw is that when he is faced with a fighter who has the knowledge and experience to nullify his elusiveness, he is forced to resort to defensive tactics that are boring and tiresome to watch. Against an inferior opponent, Whitaker is a mischievous sprite, a ring goblin whose skills can be quite entertaining. Against an opponent who is his equal, he appears to be a man who is afraid; a man who fights with survival as his primary motivation. This type of pugilist does not fill seats in large arenas. The only reason he found himself fighting in front of 70,000 people in San Antonio was that the seats were filled with Mexicans and Mexican Americans who had come to watch Julio

César Chávez challenge Sweet Pea for his WBC welterweight title.

It was a bad fight for everyone involved. Sweet Pea's vaunted elusiveness was nowhere in evidence in the early rounds. Chávez, who is deceptively quick, used lateral movement to cut off the ring and camped out on Sweet Pea's chest, pounding him to the mid-section. Things looked ominous for the Pea. In round 6, Sweet Pea did the only thing he could do to slow Chávez down—he punched him in the groin. Repeatedly. For some reason, he was not penalized for these punches, although their "clear intent," as Ferdie

Chávez nails Terrence Alli with a left hook on May 8, 1993, en route to a sixth-round knockout in Las Vegas. The victory raised Chávez's record to 87-0, including 72 knockouts.

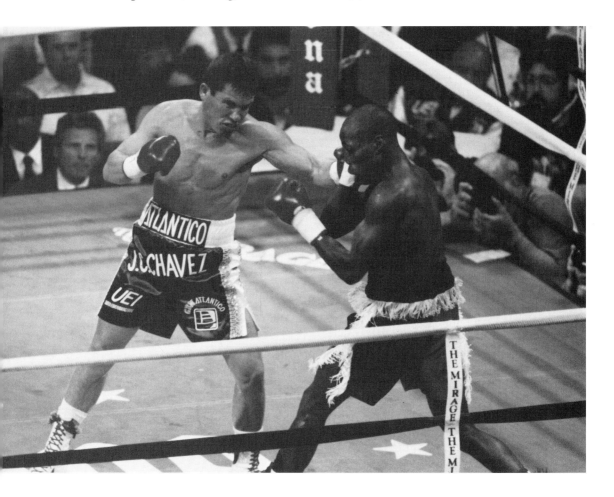

Pacheco put it, was obvious. Julio César Chávez may have an iron jaw, but in the tender areas below the belt, all men are equally vulnerable.

The low blows literally drained Chávez, as hard punches to the groin tend to do. He was in obvious agony for the next five rounds. Moving forward slowly, with his hands lowered to protect himself from further assaults below the belt, he left his face wide open. Whitaker ripped into him for the next four rounds, although he never allowed himself to get into an exchange with Chávez. Sweet Pea fought the entire fight in perpetual reverse, even when Chávez was hurt. He would halt to throw punches, then back out quickly. It was probably the longest retreat since Napoléon's forces vacated Russia. Chávez kept coming; kept pressing. He could not be stopped, at least not by the likes of Pernell Whitaker, who would have had to hit Chávez over the head with the Alamodome itself to stop him. By round 8, Chávez was beginning to recover. He signaled his return with a booming right to Whitaker's heart; the sound of the impact of the blow literally echoed off the roof of the Alamodome and left a look of wide-eyed surprise and pain on Sweet Pea's face. In round 9, Chávez started to come on strong. Sweet Pea went into full survival mode. When Chávez trapped him in a corner, Whitaker either hung onto Chávez's left arm like a drowning man or executed a truly bizarre move in which he transformed himself into a human crab, lowering himself down to the point where his haunches almost touched the canvas and scuttling away around Chávez's knees.

By round 12, Chávez seemed to be trying to drive Whitaker out of the ring by sheer pursuit. Sweet Pea propelled himself backward with the alacrity of a squid faced by a hungry shark. At times it seemed as if he was actually going to abandon the ring. Chávez never caught him.

The judges ruled the fight a draw, and Whitaker retained his title. Both fighters claimed they had won. Not surprisingly, the American press came down firmly on Whitaker's side, moving Lou Duva and Whitaker to assert they had won a "moral victory," a rather comical statement considering that Whitaker had fought one of the dirtiest fights in championship bout history. For Chávez, ultimately, it was a nonevent. He remained undefeated, and his place in boxing history was assured. He reached yet another milestone on December 18, scoring a sixth-round TKO over Andy Holligan in Puebla, Mexico. The victory gave Chávez 27 title defenses without a loss, breaking the record held by the legendary Joe Louis.

For Lou Duva, the Chávez Whitaker fight was another misadventure. Although he claimed, once again, that he had been robbed, not long after the fight he began going to great lengths to avoid a rematch. This was rather strange behavior for a man who had been shouting far and wide that his fighter had been cheated. Before he would grant Chávez a rematch, Duva proclaimed, Chávez must first declare Whitaker the winner of the first bout. Knowing that the Mexican champion would never do that, especially because Chávez believed that he had won the bout, Duva was assuring that no rematch would take place. Duva was no doubt reluctant to risk his best fighter in the ring with Chávez a second time, and Whitaker seemed to want no part of Chávez again either. He talked of being satisfied with the results, saying that the American people now knew who was truly the better fighter. Both men incorrectly assumed that Whitaker's "moral victory" would propel Sweet Pea to celebrity status, and that big fights and big paydays awaited them. But without Chávez, Whitaker was doomed to lapse into his former status as the least popular five-title champion in history. The nature of the fight he

Chávez absorbs a damaging low blow from Pernell Whitaker in round 6 of the WBC welterweight championship bout at the Alamodome in San Antonio, Texas, on September 11, 1993. The blow, one of several intentional low blows landed by Whitaker, at the instruction of Lou Duva, severely debilitated Chávez during the remains of the contest. The fight ended in a draw.

engaged in against Chávez could only hasten his return to undercard status. The sports media might proclaim Whitaker the greatest fighter since Sugar Ray Robinson, but in prizefighting, the public has the last word.

Much of the "journalism" surrounding the fight took on a disturbingly racist tone. Curiously, there were few articles that actually delved into what happened in the ring. Instead, many sportswriters launched into attacks on Chávez's character. One New York sportswriter called Chávez a "coward" for never learning to speak English and referred to him as "a worm at the bottom of a tequila bottle." Another complained that Chávez "whined" about the low blows and upbraided him for having the nerve to request a rematch.

This resentment toward Chávez, which seems to exist primarily in the media, had been building for

years. It peaked just before and after the bout with
Whitaker. Much of it no doubt has to do with
Chávez's association with the perennially reviled Don
King. But there is also something much deeper, and
far uglier, behind this resentment. Again and again,
Chávez was belittled for not speaking English. If he
had only learned to speak English, these articles and
editorials asserted, Chávez could have been the "next
Sugar Ray Leonard," hugely popular in the United
States, where he could have reaped the rewards of
commercial endorsements and talk show appearances.
These editorialists seem to have failed to ask themselves why a fighter whose ring accomplishments have
far surpassed Sugar Ray Leonard's, or any other
fighter's since Sugar Ray Robinson's, would crave soft
drink commercials and appearances with Jay Leno
when he was already a multimillionaire and a cultural
icon in his own country. What really motivated such
resentment was good, old-fashioned American chau-
vinism and, in some cases, outright racism. That same
sentiment—Why don't they learn to speak English?—can be heard daily on the street from ignorant
white Americans who fear that all non-English-
speaking people are here to steal their jobs and ruin
their neighborhoods. The difference in the forum in
which such sentiments are expressed, be it a *New York
Times Magazine* profile on a boxer from Mexico or a
street corner in Brooklyn, makes such sentiments no
less repulsive. Long-cherished notions of American
superiority over Mexico and Mexicans are turned
upside down, in the most unequivocal way, every time
Chávez steps into the ring with an American fighter,
in much the same way that cherished notions of white
superiority over blacks were challenged every time
heavyweight champion Jack Johnson demolished
some "great white hope." Julio César Chávez is a
living, breathing, slap in the face—or perhaps a left jab

to the jaw—to traditional notions of U.S. superiority over its neighbor to the south.

The media in the United States also betrays a certain jealousy of Chávez's phenomenal popularity in Mexico. The United States has no one like Julio César Chávez. Julio César Chávez is a *Mexican*. He has great pride in his country and his people. He is content with this. He still fights for the security of his family, but now his family comprises the 77 million people of Mexico. As he himself puts it, "I love them and they love me." He is Mexico's triumph, not America's. This is a hard fact for many American sports journalists to swallow. America craves a figure like Chávez—a true, untarnished hero. But Chávez is for Mexico.

CHRONOLOGY

1962	Born Julio César Chávez in Ciudad Obregón, Mexico, on July 12; family moves to Culiacán soon afterward
1978	Chávez begins to box as an amateur
1980	Engages in first professional fight, knocking out Andrés Félix on February 5, in Culiacán
1981–82	Engages in 23 bouts, winning 22 by knockout and 1 by decision; signs contract with manager Félix Ramón
1983	Fights in the United States for the first time, knocking out Roberto Sandoval in Los Angeles
1984	Wins WBC super-featherweight title with eighth-round TKO of Mario Martínez; begins association with promoter Don King
1985	Successfully defends super-featherweight title against Rubén Castillo, Roger Mayweather, and Dwight Pratchett
1986	Fights in Europe for the first time, knocking out Faustino Barrios in Paris, France; retains super-featherweight title with victories over Barrios, Refugio Rojas, Rocky Lockridge, and Juan LaPorte

1987   Wins WBA lightweight title with 11th-round
                KO of Edwin Rosario

1988   Successfully defends lightweight title against
                Rodolfo Aguilar; unifies WBA and WBC
                lightweight titles by defeating José Luis Ramírez

1989   Wins WBC super-lightweight title with
                10th-round TKO of Roger Mayweather

1990   Unifies WBC and IBF super-lightweight titles
                with 12th-round TKO of Meldrick Taylor;
                retains title with third-round KO of Kyung
                Duk Ahn

1991–92   Successfully defends super-lightweight title
                against John Duplessis, Lonnie Smith, Angel
                Hernández, Frankie Mitchell, and Hector
                Camacho

1993   Defeats Greg Haugen before 132,274 spectators
                in Aztec Stadium; retains super-lightweight title
                with sixth-round KO of Terrence Alli, raising
                his record to 87-0; junior-welterweight title
                bout with Pernell Whitaker ends in a draw;
                achieves record 27th straight title defense
                without a loss

FURTHER READING

Andre, Sam, and Nat Fleisher. *A Pictorial History of Boxing.* New York: Carol, 1990.

"A Chat with Chávez: The World's Best Fighter Speaks Out." *The Ring,* August 1993.

Hauser, Thomas. *Black Lights: Inside the World of Professional Boxing.* New York: Vintage, 1989.

"Julio César Chávez: We Answer All the Questions." *World Boxing,* October 1993.

Liebling, A. J. *The Sweet Science.* New York: Viking, 1956.

———. *In a Neutral Corner.* New York: Viking, 1969.

Nack, William. "Beaten to the Draw." *Sports Illustrated,* September 20, 1993.

Oates, Joyce Carol, and Daniel Halpurn, eds. *Reading the Fights.* New York: Prentice Hall, 1988.

Paz, Octavio. *The Labyrinth of Solitude and Other Writings.* New York: Grove Weidenfeld, 1985.

Riding, Alan. *Distant Neighbors: A Portrait of the Mexicans.* New York: Vintage, 1984.

Ryan, Jeff. "Julio César Chávez: The World's Best Fighter Is the Year's Best, Too." *The Ring,* April 1991.

Smith, Gary. "Bearing the Burden." *Sports Illustrated,* February 22, 1993.

INDEX

TERRANCE DOLAN is a freelance writer and editor and a lifelong boxing enthusiast. The editor of numerous books for young readers, he is also the author of *Probing Deep Space* in the Chelsea House WORLD EXPLORERS series and of *The Kiowa Indians* in Chelsea House's JUNIOR LIBRARY OF AMERICAN INDIANS.

RODOLFO CARDONA is professor of Spanish and comparative literature at Boston University. A renowned scholar, he has written many works of criticism, including *Ramón, a Study of Gómez de la Serna and His Works* and *Visión del esperpento: Teoría y práctica del esperpento en Valle-Inclán.* Born in San José, Costa Rica, he earned his B.A. and M.A. from Louisiana State University and received a Ph.D. from the University of Washington. He has taught at Case Western Reserve University, the University of Pittsburgh, the University of Texas at Austin, the University of New Mexico, and Harvard University.

JAMES COCKCROFT is currently a visiting professor of Latin American and Caribbean studies at the State University of New York at Albany. A three-time Fulbright scholar, he earned a Ph.D. from Stanford University and has taught at the University of Massachusetts, the University of Vermont, and the University of Connecticut. He is the author or coauthor of numerous books on Latin American subjects, including *Neighbors in Turmoil: Latin America, The Hispanic Experience in the United States: Contemporary Issues and Perspectives,* and *Outlaws in the Promised Land: Mexican Immigrant Workers and America's Future.*